Kindly Bent to Ease Us

Klong-chen rab-'byams-pa

Part Three: Wonderment
sGyu-ma ngal-gso

from

The Trilogy of Finding Comfort and Ease
Ngal-gso skor-gsum

Translated from the Tibetan and annotated by

Herbert V. Guenther

Dharma Publishing

TIBETAN TRANSLATION SERIES

Copyright © 1976 by Dharma Publishing
Printed in the United States of America.
All rights reserved. No part of this book
may be reproduced in any form without written
permission. For information address:
Dharma Publishing, 2425 Hillside Ave.,
Berkeley, California 94704

Illustrations:
Frontispiece: rDo-rje sems-dpa' (Vajrasattva),
the embodiment of the five Dhyāni Buddhas
Page 2: 'Jigs-med gling-pa: Great Nyingma lama
known as the second Klong-chen-pa
Page 76: Ral-gcig-ma (Ekajatī), a Dharmapāla
Page 172: Stūpa, a symbol
of the Mind of the Buddha

ISBN: 0-913546-44-5; 0-913546-45-3 (pbk)
Library of Congress Number: 75-29959

Typeset in Fototronic Elegante and
printed by Dharma Press

9 8 7 6

To Tarthang Tulku Rinpoche

Contents

Foreword

Longchenpa (1308–1363) was recognized as a supreme visionary by all the schools of Tibetan Buddhism, particularly the Nyingma. Through his erudite writings, he has made available a most comprehensive understanding of the way to enlightenment. The depth of his exploration and knowledge of Dharma texts exceeded all of his predecessors in Tibet, and like the Mahāyāna masters of India, his contributions were a milestone for the intellectual tradition of Buddhism. Through his writings, he carefully explains the essence of the Buddha's teachings by integrating an inconceivably wide variety of teachings in order to more clearly delineate the path to enlightenment. He has accomplished this not by philosophizing, but by giving illuminating descriptions based upon practical experience.

Like the Lam-rim literature of other schools, this trilogy is basically a discourse on how to enter the enlightenment path. It is not necessarily written from the highest viewpoint, as are the other volumes of Longchenpa's 'Seven Treasuries', yet it consists of the nectar or essence of literally thousands of texts. For the Nyingma, this series has the purpose of preparing the student for the higher teachings of Mahā, Anu, and Atiyoga. In our tradition, such a preparatory stage is called *sngon-'gro*. The purpose of the *sngon-'gro* is to explain how to enter the path consisting of the starting-point (*gzhi*), path (*lam*), and goal (*'bras-bu*). Wherever a person is along the path, these texts demonstrate that the nature of reality is unchanged.

During my study in Tibet, before I had to leave the area of Golok and travel to the central provinces, I was fortunate to intensively study and practice these texts with some of the most learned living masters of the Nyingmapa, such as Tarthang mChog-sprul and Ā-'gyur Rinpoche, as well as the second 'Jam-dbyangs-mkhyen-brtse'i-dbang-po, Chos-kyi blo-gros. These lineages of oral-transmission pass through Longchenpa and continue uninterrupted to Padmasambhava, and ultimately to the Ādibuddha, Kun-tu bzang-po.

This translation by my dear friend Dr. Guenther is a most successful way of presenting to the Western world these valuable writings. In the past, there have not been very many acceptable translations of Buddhist psychological terms because of the lack of a suitable conceptual language. Perhaps in the future more accurate translations will occur, when the internal experiences described in these texts have been made more alive in the West.

Finally, I would like to dedicate this book to all of my friends who have been so supportive and who have given me the opportunity to bring my own tradition of Tibetan Buddhism to this country. The completion of this trilogy makes me particularly joyous, for now we have the Oral-transmission Lineage and the translated texts. The seeds have been planted. For the last seven years while in America, I have hoped that this dream—of making these fundamental Buddhist teachings available—would come true. Without Dr. Guenther's dedication or the stamina of the workers at Dharma Press, this project would never have been possible. To them I am forever grateful.

Nyingma Institute   Tarthang Tulku Rinpoche
Berkeley, California

Preface

ach of the three parts of Klong-chen rab-'byams-pa's monumental *Trilogy of Finding Comfort and Ease* is unique in being complete in itself, and yet there exists between them a subtle interrelationship which prevents this completeness from becoming 'closed'. Each completeness is, strange to say, an 'openness' that allows the person dealing with the topics discussed to extend his relation with his world and, at the same time, to expand the horizon of his understanding and to enlarge the range of his actions. In this process the person is seen as not so much seeking for truth, but as letting the internal logic of Being shine forth, and this logic then becomes the 'sense' or 'truth' of his life, coloring in subtle hues his particular 'world' which represents the meaning he has found. This 'sense' may be said to be the feeling of wonderment, not so much as a passive state, but as an active, and, in the strict sense of the word, a creative manner of looking at our familiar world, as if it were for the first time. In wonderment we can see with enormous clarity and exquisite sensitivity. This is quite different from the manner in our 'waking' state which is essentially one of inhibition and which in its routine dullness lacks luster and inspiration. There is thus an intimate connection between 'dreaming' (with which Klong-chen rab-'byams-pa begins his work) as a process which assists a person in shaping his life, and 'wonderment' as the same process raised to a higher level from which again it may influence our capacities for overcoming the monotony of ordinary restricted visions. In the treatment of the various shapes this creative process may take, Klong-chen rab-'byams-pa, as in his other works, reveals his quality as an independent thinker.

The internal logic of Being as an ongoing opening-up for 'meaning', which is experienced existentially through the symbols which we call man's passage through life as a task and quest, is mediated through Mind as the fundamental ground of experience and of being, without ever being *a* mind or *a* being. This existential experience of Being (*chos-sku*) through Mind (*sems-nyid*) is the theme of the first part of the *Trilogy*. The mediation process (*bsam-gtan*), popularly referred to as 'meditation', but interpreted by Klong-chen rab-'byams-pa from quite a different angle, is a probing of the very horizon in and through which the internal logic of Being reveals itself by radiating into all beings and thereby allows us as beings to participate in it (*longs-sku*). This is the theme of the second part. The shaping of this horizon into concrete and intelligible forms (*sprul-sku*), as a process of what from one angle seems to be an enchantment and from another pure wonderment (*sgyu-ma*), is the theme of the third part. It thus presupposes the other two parts which, in turn, lead to this part. Each part reflects a certain level of organization which is complete in itself but reveals its meaning only in interpenetration with the others.

As in his previous works Klong-chen rab-'byams-pa has structured each chapter in a distinct manner. But only in the first chapter has he detailed the practicing of the topic under discussion. In the remaining chapters he merely refers to the analysis given in the first chapter. The structuring is here indicated in the same way as in the previous volumes.

Without the help and encouragement of my dear friend Tarthang Tulku it would not have been possible to complete a work of this nature, and I gratefully acknowledge his invaluable advice.

I am grateful to my colleagues and friends, professors Keith Scott and Leslie S. Kawamura, for critical comments, and above all to my wife for her unfailing support.

Everyone who consults the Index, which includes the indices of Part One and Part Two, so as to provide cross-references as well as to indicate differences in interpretation of technical terms due to the context in which they are used, will be grateful to Mr. James Trites.

Finally, I wish to thank the editorial staff of Dharma Publishing, Mr. Steven D. Goodman and, particularly, Miss Judy Robertson for careful and skilled editing.

Saskatoon/Berkeley   Herbert V. Guenther

Kindly Bent to Ease Us

Introduction

The third and final part of Klong-chen rab-'byams-pa's 'Trilogy of Finding Comfort and Ease' (*Ngal-gso skor-gsum*) might easily be characterized and re-titled as 'Variations on the Theme of Being', where each variation is a modulation of one of the eight aspects or facets of Being as stated by Nāgārjuna in the opening stanza of his Madhyamakakārikās. But while Nāgārjuna's statement remains prosaic and coldly intellectual, Klong-chen rab-'byams-pa's presentation is permeated by the warmth of felt knowledge and the rich imagery that can derive only from a most intimate and immediate experience. His work, therefore, appeals directly and strongly to the imagination as the primary capacity to bring to light significant meanings by which life is enriched, if not fulfilled.

As in the other parts of the Trilogy, Klong-chen rab-'byams-pa views the structure of being human—seen as an active process—as a narrowing and shifting of the horizon of Being. As a horizon, Being is both an openness and meaningfulness; it involves a cognitive agency for which meaningfulness becomes an experienced presence made possible by openness as an opening-up. In this sense it is possible to speak of the identity of Being and thinking in a very special manner, identity not being merely an equation. Several steps are necessary to grasp the full import of this problem which is central to rDzogs-chen thought and which gives Klong-chen rab-'byams-pa's discussion its specific flavor. First of all, Being is not *a* being, an empty generality or 'category', contrasted with and limited by other beings. It is, rather, an openness which, as a dynamic process, sets up, and is felt and known as, a presence. Since there is no presence without a response, the act of responding may be called the process of 'thinking'. The process of thinking displays a double role. The one (A) is 'thinking Being itself' in utter openness and, for want of a more adequate term, may be said to be a 'pristine cognition' (*ye-shes*), a cognition that has been operative since a beginningless beginning in bringing out the meaningfulness of Being.[1] Hence it is not passively receptive but actively informative, and has its very dynamic in the cognitive property of Being itself (*rig-pa*) which, for want of a better term, may be rendered as 'the cognitive property of Being' or, in an epistemological context where it is frequently used, as an 'intrinsic or pure awareness' (*rig-pa*). In its response to Being this thinking remains actively open, while also allowing itself to be permeated by openness.

The other role displayed by the process of thinking (B) is 'thinking about *a* being'. It tends to become closed and impervious to Being as a live presence, and in dealing with a being it loses its own character of pristineness and ultimately is lacking in pure cognitiveness. This loss and lack of pure cognitiveness and pristineness is characteristic of the mind as a noetic-noematic complex. In other words, because of Being's dynamic character—a sheer occurring—presenting itself as thinking, Being is transmuted in this process into *a* being, that is, some kind of being, and 'intrinsic awareness', 'Mind-as-such', into *a* mind which by force of the 'gravitational pull' of its complexity becomes ever more involved in the noematic contents of its own making and, in the strict sense of the word, is a lessening of the awareness or cognitiveness (*ma-rig-pa*) that is both Being and of Being.

If Being is inseparable from Awareness (thinking) and vice versa, it is a rather artificial procedure, adopted nevertheless by traditional philosophy, to deal with them separately as if they were independent entities. However, by stating that Being is not *a* being and that Mind-as-such, Awareness, is not *a* mind, that is, by pointing out what the meaning of these concepts is not, the way is paved for a positive understanding of the dynamic unity of Being-Awareness, and only the necessity of a clarifying discussion imposes a separate treatment of Being and of Awareness which ultimately will reconfirm the inseparability of the two concepts fused into a single dynamic notion for which the term 'ground' (*gzhi*) is used. This term corresponds in Western terminology to the idea of 'Being' which since the beginning of metaphysics has shown itself as having the character of ground as the first and most universal ground of all beings and which, like its counterpart *gzhi*, has lent itself to a static interpretation.[2] Therefore, to retain such terms as 'ground' or 'Being' poses a certain risk because each term embodies possible misconstruances. This risk is minimized if we bear in mind that rDzogs-chen thought, as elaborated by Klong-chen rab-'byams-pa, does not share in the substantialist prejudice of traditional philosophies (East *and* West), but is concerned with the dynamic wholeness of reality which makes any reductionism impossible.

This single dynamic notion of 'ground' sums up the indivisibility and inseparability of what is termed 'initially pure' (*ka-dag*) which is descriptive of 'facticity' (*ngo-bo*), the 'pure fact of Being' as experienced, rather than as an intellectual abstraction, on the one hand, and what is termed 'spontaneously given' (*lhun-grub*), which is descriptive of 'actuality' (*rang-bzhin*), the 'existential immediacy of Being', on the other, each of them being further characterized as 'open-dimensional' (*stong-pa*) and 'radiant' (*gsal-ba*), respectively. Despite the noun-adjective pattern of language with its suggestiveness of substance and quality and the attendant division into static phenomena (things) and dynamic phenomena (motions), the summary notion of 'ground' highlights the impossibility of applying to this idea the traditional analytical concepts of Western philosophy as well as, where processes are involved, the classical corpuscular-kinetic framework with its assumption of substance and motion—the former immutable and permanent, the latter a mere displacement of the former within a pre-existent and static space. Moreover, the difficulty that attends any formulation of a synthetic judgment, because our ordinary thinking is conditioned by analytical habits, is enhanced and made even more complex by the inclusion of a third element, 'pure or intrinsic awareness' or, like the other attributes taken descriptively, 'tendential' as a pure cognitive property (*rig-pa*). This property has nothing to do with subjective mind, but is again illustrative of 'responsiveness' or 'resonance' (*thugs-rje*) on which understanding depends. It thus refers to an ever-present act of selecting which verges on ending a state of indeterminacy. The inclusion of this third element emphasizes the evidence of our immediate experience as primary. Experience has to do with meanings and values that are brought to light through experiencing them as constituting the realities of the universe. Therefore, 'intelligence' is intrinsic to Being, not its derivative. This complex and complicated 'primordial state' or 'ground', as detailed above, is concisely described by Klong-chen rab-'byams-pa in the following words:

> Facticity which is initially pure is inseparable (from actuality) because the latter's spontaneous givenness is there as an intense radiance from out of its depth (or facticity) to the cognitive property (*rig-pa*) of facticity initially pure, and not found as substance or quality; the subtle lucency of actuality which is spontaneously given, is present as an inner glow, so

that while the very facticity of presence remains open-dimensional (*stong-pa*), the actuality of what is open-dimensional is radiant (*gsal-ba*), and the very intrinsicality of radiance is its cognitive property (*rig-pa*). Hence (experientially) a founding stratum or existentiality (*sku*) and a founded pristine cognitiveness (*ye-shes*), having been such from the very beginning that the one cannot be added to or subtracted from the other, are present like the very nature of the sun (and its light). In this way the inseparability of actuality, spontaneously given, from facticity initially pure, is established.[3]

In order to understand the complexity of what is summarily referred to as 'ground' or, in Western philosophical terminology, 'Being', the following diagrammatical analysis may be of some help.[4]

The facticity of Being (*ngo-bo*) is nowhere else than in its actuality (*rang-bzhin*) which as a dynamic presence elicits a response to its solicitations, thus implying an interactional exchange of information between itself and responsiveness (*thugs-rje*). Moreover, facticity as facticity precedes, though not temporally, any conceptual framework into which it might be pressed, and any attempt to characterize this facticity can only be made by the descriptive phrase of it being 'initially pure' (*ka-dag*). If facticity is nowhere else than in its actuality, it follows that it must be 'spontaneously given' (*lhun-grub*) and as such is 'totalistic' (*kun-khyab*) in every respect. In the form of a diagram this is

ngo-bo (*ka-dag*)

$$\|$$

rang-bzhin (*lhun-grub*) $\longleftarrow \, - - - - - \longrightarrow$ *thugs-rje* (*kun-khyab*)

This ontological status of Being on the level of experience, already intimated by the inclusion of responsiveness, is such that its facticity has an 'open-dimensional quality' or, as we may say, is an 'openness' (*stong-pa*) which in its actuality is 'radiant' or present as 'lucency', 'radiance', 'radiation' (*gsal-ba*), which in view of its active character of sending messages by radiation is responded to by a 'pure cognition' (*rig-pa*), which is the cognitive property of Being itself. More concretely speaking, the open-dimensional facticity becomes man's 'existentiality' (*sku*) which is not a rigid entity or an eternal substance, but an openness that sends its messages through 'communication' (*gsung*) in the sense that its radiation communicates itself to and is being responded to by an 'aliveness' which is man's 'spirituality' (*thugs*). A diagram, corresponding to and reflecting the ontological diagram above, but illustrating the process of experience, is

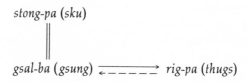

A further exploration shows that the above belongs to the prereflective phase of experience as yet undisturbed by reflective discrimination which, of course, is already latently at work, and in the explicit reflective phase gives rise to such predications as that man's concrete being is 'existential' (*sku-yin*), that the existentiality that communicates itself to others is a 'lighting-up' (*'od-yin*), and that the cognitive property of this aliveness is a 'pristine cognition' (*ye-shes-yin*). However, whatever 'reflection' is at work in this prereflective phase is not yet vitiated by habitual quantification and reductionist interpretations. The upshot of this analysis is that 'Being' or 'ground' does not involve a quantitative view of reality, but remains qualitative through and through, because of its experiential character and its inherent meaningfulness.

Elsewhere Klong-chen rab-'byams-pa speaks of 'ground' as a 'primordial ground in general' (*thog-ma'i spyi-gzhi*)[5] and elaborates on it:

Before there was the emergence of a state of being a Buddha through an inner understanding, and before there developed a state of being an (ordinary) sentient being through lack of an inner understanding, there existed, objectively, a continuum of meanings, open-dimensional and 'making room' like the vault of the bright sky; bright and unquavering like the depth of the ocean; shining and unceasingly making 'room' like the surface of a stainless mirror.[6] In the center of (what may be said to be) the very meaningfulness (of reality) there resides its intrinsicality, a cognitive property that maintains (its inseparability from) the ground as facticity, actuality and responsiveness. Furthermore, since it is not predetermined as Saṃsāra, it unceasingly makes room for the emergence of Saṃsāra (and in this respect is) like camphor; and since it also is not predetermined as Nirvāṇa, it unceasingly makes room for the emergence of Nirvāṇa (and hence also is) like camphor. Although its facticity is not pre-determined in any way, it assumes different qualities under certain conditions. While the ground has neither defects nor qualities, as a mere possibility for the emergence (of distinct qualities), it is like the Wish-fulfilling Gem because it may develop into anything one chooses, and hence it exists as the ultimate primeval source of all and everything. In the *Kun-gsal*[7] it is stated:

Before there was any development or origination
There existed the primordial Lord 'Immutable Light'[8]
As the ultimate primeval source of all and everything,
Like the sky, the ocean, a jewel, camphor.

And,

Before there was any development or origination,
Before there developed the state of being a Buddha,
    by understanding
Or that of an ordinary sentient being by lack of
    understanding,
Or the existence of both,
There was the primordial Lord 'Immutable Light'
Who had spontaneously realized Buddhahood.
He existed like a rainbow in the sky,
A sheer lucency and hence not something eternally
    non-existent,[9]

An utter insubstantiality and hence not something
eternally existent.[10]
He existed as the ultimate primeval source of all
and everything.
In having become the concrete ground of all and
everything
He remained an unlimited vastness and he also did
not allow of any partition,
And he existed spontaneously in inseparability (of
facticity and actuality).

Moreover, the facticity of this self-existent pristine cognitiveness (which is the dynamic of) the cognitive property (of
Being) is like a jewel because it has been spontaneously there
from the very beginning. Since it is not predetermined as
either Saṃsāra or Nirvāṇa but unceasingly under the conditions of understanding or lack of understanding, it therefore is
like camphor, which also is not predetermined as to beneficial
or harmful properties, but unceasingly makes room for the
emergence of its beneficial or harmful properties under the
respective conditions of diseases due to heat or cold. The very
cognitive property (of Being) which is not found as anything
(or anywhere), when it gives itself ground for the emergence of
any (quality) under favorable conditions, is termed thereness
of ground, which in itself is neither good nor bad, neither steps
out of itself nor turns into something other than itself. It is a
matter of marvel.[11]

This lengthy passage which basically restates the single
dynamic notion of 'ground' and which by its last sentence
brings to mind Martin Heidegger's dictum that 'mystery
adheres to the very nature of Being', has a certain onto-
theological character so prevalent in traditional metaphysics.
Ontology thinks of Being as the first and universal ground
common to all beings and theology thinks of Being as the
highest ground above all beings. However, a closer inspection reveals that the 'ground' as detailed in rDzogs-chen
thought leads out of metaphysics to where the onto-theolog-

ical speculation of metaphysics has its origin, thus anticipating Heidegger's later thinking.[12] Another, even more important point is that this single dynamic notion abolishes the traditional distinction between space and the stuff that fills it, thus being in accord with modern physics. Space, metaphorically termed the sky, is not an indifferent and empty container, but a dynamic opening process, quite literally making room for its local spatiotemporal modifications. This opening-up, therefore, is not something occurring *in* something, but simply an opening-up. Next, the analogy with the Wish-fulfilling Gem points to the 'act of selection' by which a certain way of living in the world as a horizon of meaning becomes established. Lastly, the reference to camphor having an ambivalent character in medicinal use has a wider implication than this and is suggestive of a compound model of the universe, which remains dynamic.[13]

While the concept of 'ground' is basically related to an ontological problem, its wider connotation in rDzogs-chen thought leads directly into the cosmological problem which involves an experiencer for whom there is a 'world' of which he is part, and by which he is acted upon as much as he is acting upon it. It is merely from an analytical approach that the 'actuality' or 'spontaneous givenness', the existential immediacy of the ground or Being, commands greater attention. It has to be emphasized over and again that all these terms have a dynamic meaning. The 'spontaneous givenness' comes as an indeterminacy in so far as, on the one hand, it points back to what may be said to be an internal change in the 'facticity' of the ground which seems to have occurred in the manner of a contingent, not a necessary event whose irreducible chance character manifests a basic indeterminacy.[14] On the other hand, the 'spontaneous givenness' also provides the chance to end this state of indeterminacy in one way or another. Chance, therefore, is not a mere random fluctuation, but involves a selective principle for and within a process generating its own norms. That there is no predetermination whatsoever and that the norms (Saṃ-sāra and Nirvāṇa) evolve within the process is evident from such statements as

> Kun-tu bzang-po, without ever having done the slightest good, has realized Buddhahood by recognizing the three (facets of Being) for what they are. The sentient beings in the three realms, without ever having done any evil, roam about in Saṃsāra by not having recognized the three facets for what they are. They roam about in Saṃsāra because they have failed to recognize facticity to be open-dimensional, actuality to be radiant, and responsiveness to be (the unity of) presence (presentation) and openness.[15]

The internal change which presents itself as 'radiance' or 'lucency' or 'radiation' might be likened to radioactive dis-integration which also occurs spontaneously and indepen-dently of any extranuclear factors. The radiation that is thus set free is technically referred to as 'the ground's self-presentation' or self-manifestation or self-actualization (*gzhi-snang*),[16] and, as this technical term implies, 'Being' comes in its totality and not merely in parts and pieces. Apart from its implication of a total self-manifestation, this term already has certain epistemological overtones since presentation is to be present to, present itself to a responding process. Therefore, it could be rendered technically as 'phenomenal-ity' as well. Another term, often used simultaneously with the above one, is 'spontaneously given' (*lhun-grub*). This term preserves more the ontological character of the 'ground' or 'Being', but it, too, because of its association with experi-ence, has an immediate bearing on human existence. Only from this totalistic overview will Klong-chen rab-'byams-pa's discussion become intelligible. He states:

> Within the primordial continuum (as) an existential energy reservoir that remains forever fresh,[17] facticity is present as existentiality, actuality as communication, and responsiveness as spirituality. By virtue of the fact that what is to become the

radiation of the five (kinds of) motility as pristine cognitions, in conjunction with the four vitalizing forces which are present as a pure cognitive property,[18] becomes outward directed, the wall of the existential energy reservoir is broken through. Together with the presence of five light values, each like a spark of fire, issuing from the now outward-directed glow of the spontaneous givenness (as which the ground is presently available), the outward-directed glow of responsiveness as a pure cognitive property becomes the very cognitive capacity that is going to deal with observable qualities (phenomena), and this (latter capacity) is present as 'loss of intrinsic awareness' (*ma-rig-pa*) which is so called with reference to the (original) pure cognitive property due to the fact that the former is no longer cognizant of itself as to what it is in itself. At this stage of the process, when there is the emergence of the ground's self-presentation, there seems to occur something like a change although the 'ground' itself does not undergo any change and this is termed 'presentation to cognitions'. At this moment the presence (-presentation) of the initially pure (facticity of Being) is like a cloudless sky, and out of its reach and range there come self-presentationally the eight procedures through which the spontaneous givenness (of Being) is manifested. The presentation of this thereness of a precious casket is such (i) that by unceasingly making room for what seems to be responsiveness, compassion arises in sentient beings; (ii) that by unceasingly making room for what seems to be a light value, the self-lucency of pristine cognitiveness fills the whole presence like a rainbow; (iii) that by unceasingly making room for what seems to be pristine cognition, there is a staying in a realm in which no divisive concepts enter; (iv) that by unceasingly making room for what seems to be like (individual) existences, the whole sky is filled by the luminous embodiment of peaceful and fearful divine forces; (v) that by unceasingly making room for what seems to be non-duality, there is no discursiveness as to whether (what is there) is one or many; (vi) that by unceasingly making room for what seems to be unlimitedness, the spontaneous givenness of Being is radiant in its own presence; (vii) that by unceasingly making room for what seems to be the gateway for pristine cognitions, the pure (aspect of Being), the presence of facticity, initially pure, is seen above like the cloudless sky; and (viii) that by unceasingly making room for what seems to be the gateway to Saṃsāra, the impure (aspect of Being),[19] below the presence of the six kinds of sentient beings present themselves, as is stated in the (semistanza):

> Saṃsāra with its evil forms of life has manifested itself from the very beginning in a playful manner.

Thus, although there are countless manifestations of founding strata of full engagement in a world-horizon, (which is) the fields of the five founded (kinds) of pristine cognitions, deriving from the creativity of the self-presentation of the spontaneous givenness (of Being), they all are (experienced as) shining in their own light in front of (the experiencer). The manifestations of the fields for the founding strata of meaning taking concrete shape within the experiencer's world-horizon, that appear in-between the (above five) horizons out of the creativity of the capabilities (constituting the spontaneous givenness of Being), also present themselves in countless numbers. And what presents itself as the sentient beings below, out of the creativity of responsiveness, also presents itself self-presentationally in countless numbers. While in this way the ground's self-presentation, manifesting itself brightly and directly, is like the appearance of an image in a mirror, this presentation is a presentation to itself and to no one else, but in not knowing that it is a presentation to itself, it occurs like a dream-presence, indistinctly glimmering, evanescent, fleeting, and it lasts only a moment since it cannot be held in itself.[20]

To a certain extent this passage is highly technical. Therefore, in order to understand the process nature of the self-manifestation of the ground or, using a different technical diction, of Being becoming being—which implies the inseparability of space from time, and throughout exhibits a dynamic unity of time-space that does away with the idea of and the belief in a processless container—it may be helpful to follow this process step by step.

The starting point is what is termed 'the facticity of Being, absolutely pure in itself from a beginning that has had no beginning' (*gdod-ma'i ka-dag chen-po*).[21] Being was already there before the split into Saṃsāra and Nirvāṇa, as distinct features, occurred. Insofar as Being involves experience, it is already an 'objective' continuum of meanings that in its presence is pure, an open dimension, defying any propositions about it. It also is lucent and radiant without its radiance being concretely tangible, and it is equally cognitive without there being the necessity to resort to concepts. By way of analogy it is like the clear autumn sky and, since experience is directly involved and cannot be detached from it, it is encountered by the cognitive capacity in a state of utter composure. In modern terms, which still are geared to a universe that fights shy of experience, this starting-point may be likened to 'zero energy' or 'primary inner' motion,[22] which sets the scene for the first phase (A), the self-presentation of a 'spontaneous givenness precious as such' (*lhun-grub rin-po-che*).[23] This now is an outward-directed radiation which in its facticity (aspect) retains the open-dimensional character of Being and which in its actuality (aspect) remains lucent and radiant, but which in its responsiveness (aspect) that assumes the outward glow of pure cognitiveness presents itself in a variety of light values which are as yet not concretized into distinct 'colors' by the responding cognitiveness. By way of analogy it is like the appearance of a rainbow in a clear sky or the sheen of brocade.

The second phase (B) is a total presence (*gzhi-snang chen-po*)[24] in which above, below and everywhere there are manifested the realms of what is experienced as calm or angry forces. This total presence also is radiant, but its light is sometimes more brilliant, sometimes more opaque; there is an emission of rays of light, rather than a steady glow. By way of analogy it is an array of maṇḍalas of calm and angry deities. The third phase (C) is the presence of what the experiencer is going to 'feel' in becoming a founding stratum of a total engagement in a world-horizon (*longs-sku'i snang-ba*)[25] which in all regions comes as a realm of affinities. But this presence remains 'above', upward-directed, while directly in front of the experiencer it is about to take concrete shape as the experiencer's world-horizon, which then imperceptibly fuses with the fourth phase (D) which is downward-directed, but which at first remains a guiding principle embodying itself in the forms of the 'Buddhas' for the six kinds of beings in the world, and then, on the most concrete level of ordinary existence, is the presence of concrete 'Buddhas' as 'lights from another world', as we might say figuratively, while at the same time reminding us of the fact that the 'light' is yet present in us.

The repeated reference to 'founding strata'—a technical term that may at first seem to be rather forbidding because of its analytical implications where synthetic formulations are involved—highlights the significance which experience plays in this dynamic process of becoming. The founding strata have to do with man's 'existentiality' (*sku*) which is indissolubly fused with Being but has meaning only in and through experience. Existentiality is Being experienced, but since Being is always becoming, man himself is a process passing through various stages that remain 'layered' or spatial while simultaneously being temporal through experience. This dynamic unity of time-space is clearly evident in Klong-chen rab-'byams-pa's concise summary of this process:

> Below as well as after (*'og-tu*) what has presented itself to be like a cloudless sky, from out of the initially pure (*ka-dag*), (the pure fact or facticity of Being), there makes itself felt, from among the eight possibilities in which the spontaneous givenness (*lhun-grub*) of Being presents itself, a pristine cognitiveness (which involves the feeling of there being) a founding stratum for the engagement (of this pristine cognitiveness) in a world-horizon (*longs-sku*); and from out of the creativity (of this complex) there presents itself, from among the immense pos-

sibilities that each of the five affinities (with Being) holds, directly in front of the experiencer, (the experience of the experiencer being) a founding stratum for a more specific and concrete world-horizon that still is the actuality of Being (*rang-bzhin sprul-sku*). Down below comes the realm of the six kinds of sentient beings, each having its own specific 'teacher' (who is a concrete founding stratum for the meanings that make sense to the particular kind of beings) (*sprul-sku*). This self-presentation of three founding strata that comes in three layers, is the self-manifestation of the ground (Being) in its spontaneous givenness.[26]

The identification of 'existentiality' with a 'teacher' in the context of a concrete world, such as the world of man, implies that it is the idea of humanity, as we would say, shining through those who remain inalienated from Being, which acts as the guiding principle for those aspiring to find their 'humanity'. The concepts of 'within' and 'without' lose all their analytical connotations by having become fused in the single dynamic notion of process.

This passage which must be seen in connection with the previous ones, is significant in many respects, apart from once again underlining the fact that our ordinary analytic concepts cannot do full justice to what is said in the texts. First of all, the passage singles out the 'positive' and ordering process which in itself reveals a complexity of meanings. On the other hand, this process evolves out of and presents the indeterminacy of the spontaneous givenness of Being, which therefore seems to be 'objective' and not merely a 'subjective' inability. Actually, neither 'subjective' nor 'objective' have any meaning in themselves in this context, because the inherent cognitive property of the totality in which Being presents itself to itself shares in the general indeterminacy and gradually evolves either into a pristine cognition, or into the lack of pure awareness. Rather than being a deficiency, the very indeterminacy holds a tremendous richness that has prompted those who have had this experience to term the spontaneous givenness 'precious' and to compare it with a jewel box. Without pressing the analogy too far, it might be suggested that in this context man (who remains process) is both a 'closed system' and, simultaneously, because of his embeddedness in the wider field of Being, a 'dissipative structure'. The indeterminacy that is resolved by an act of selection that is either truly cognitive (*rig-pa*) or less so (*ma-rig-pa*) is illustrated by the simile of camphor which for many centuries has been used as a medicine. In the words of Klong-chen rab-'byams-pa:

> In the same way as camphor, which is beneficial in cases of disease due to heat, but harmful in cases of disease due to cold, is in itself neither beneficial nor harmful, so also the 'ground' and the 'ground's self-manifestation' appear to be beneficial, in the presence of what is a condition for finding freedom, by those who recognize the two for what they are, but if they are not recognized for what they are, they appear to be harmful due to each of their aspects being made a starting point for becoming mistaken about them. The ground and its self-manifestation are in no way pre-existent as virtue or defect.[27]

Consequently,

> The state of a Buddha, and that of a sentient being, is merely the recognition or non-recognition of the presence (of Being) for what it is. Saṃsāra and Nirvāṇa (are judgments that) have a common cause in the cognitive property (of Being) and are like the palm and the back of a hand.[28]

Not only is the ground's self-presentation and self-manifestation thoroughly dynamic, and in its movement may be said to be as elusive and evanescent as a dream, it also is fluctuational, though not as a random process. If it is recognized for what it is, it leads to higher levels of organization and ultimately, over and above them, to itself; if not, it gives rise to increased frustration. This fluctuational character is indicated by Klong-chen rab-'byams-pa:

> The totality of the ground's self-presentation that comes out of its ground may or may not be recognized for what it is. It

passes like the luster of a crystal dissolving in the crystal, or like a previous dream image fading away with the emergence of a subsequent dream image. The ground's presence (presentation) disappearing in what is nothing as such means it does not go anywhere else, but returns to its initial glow (tending to become outward directed again) in the same way as a dream does not go anywhere but dissolves in sleep. Or, even more conspicuously, when one awakens, the dream merely disappears in the (general) cognitive process, but does not go anywhere else.[29]

The indeterminacy that marks the ground's self-presentation reveals two contrasting, rather than opposing, tendencies which have certain features in common in that they are finalistic in the formal sense of moving towards a final state without involving a 'final cause'. In the passages that have been quoted above, they are referred to as 'gateways'. The one leads to Saṃsāra which, quite literally, is felt as a state in which one is 'running around in circles', always coming to a dead end. The other opens up to fresh vistas and is felt as relief and release (Nirvāṇa). As such this tendency is 'formative' in the sense that it leads to a new dynamic regime. The formative tendency, therefore, is positive and actually predominates in living systems which tend towards higher-order organization. This tendency is concerned with values such as the emergence of compassion which passes beyond mere utilitarian criteria; with colors, not so much as pigments but as vibrating light values, the luminous understructure of what is to become ordinary 'reality';[30] with forms and embodiments to hold and express feelings and emotions; with freshness of vision and cognition that remains appreciative; with unity rather than fragmentation; and, lastly, with meaningfulness of being, a meaningfulness that knows no bounds and remains irreducible to preconceived or postulated entities.

Strictly speaking this formative tendency is the very creativity that is otherwise termed the 'responsiveness' of the ground in its presence as a cognitive property, and it operates in the threefold mode of creativity, adornment, and playfulness. The unitary character of this triple mode Klong-chen rab-'byams-pa describes as follows:

> Creativity, adornment, and playfulness exist in (and as) an inner (experienceable) continuum, a spontaneous, precious system, the ground and the ground's self-presentation. As such they begin to radiate outwardly, just as in a mirror the image of a face appears. How do they exist in the inner continuum? Creativity does so because within the very nature of the cognitive property (of the ground in its presentation) which is open-dimensional, it unceasingly makes room for its formative manifestation. Adornment does so (by virtue of the fact) that the open-dimensionality is not an absolute nothingness and hence is an adornment that is pristine cognitiveness; that the spontaneous givenness is not something inert and hence is an adornment that is clear and insubstantial, and that its outward directed glow is neither something material nor just nothing, but is beautified by its cognitive quality. Playfulness does so (by virtue of the fact that) the cognitive property plays in its own outward directed glow, that this outward directed glow plays in pristine cognition, and that from this playfulness there comes the play of incipient outward radiation. These three modes are not something other than the cognitive property of the ground. When these three modes are understood they are called 'capabilities', because the greatness of cognitiveness becomes thus manifest.[31]

It is through this creativity of the cognitive property of Being, qualifying, as it were, its aspects of responsiveness, which is as much a process adding beauty to what is going on as it is a playful dance, that the self-manifestation of Being, which at first seems to proceed dream-like—the process of dreaming being the ongoing self-mirroring of Being—acquired its magical character of weaving its spells that turn into either the enchantment in Saṃsāra or the wonderment of pristine cognition in Nirvāṇa. This intimate relationship between dreaming (*rmi-lam*) and wizardry (*sgyu-ma*), the one more 'passive', the other more 'active', and thus like every dynamic whole constituting a synthesis of contraries, sets the opening scene of Klong-chen rab-'byams-pa's dissertation.

The indeterminacy of what is otherwise termed the ground's (or Being's) self-manifestation and self-presentation to itself, for reasons stated above, as a spontaneous givenness, soliciting and receiving (strictly within itself because of its totalistic character) a response that will end the indeterminacy, nevertheless involves the indeterminacy of the response, precisely because the responding aspect shares in the general indeterminacy. There have always been attempts to explain this indeterminacy away in order to save a static or (when this steady-state view of the world ran into difficulties) a cyclical universe. And yet experience at every stage contradicts and invalidates any staticness. In other words, the response may be 'positive' and may carry with it the feeling of enrichment, if not fulfillment, or it may be 'negative', carrying with it the feeling of impoverishment and frustration—in terms of cognition, becoming lost in confusion and conflict.

This theme of becoming lost has found its expression in allegorical language in the *Rig-pa rang-shar chen-po'i rgyud*:

> Friends, although in pure Buddhahood there is no losing one's way, the manner in which rDo-rje sems-dpa' became lost in his own domain was as follows: He strayed from his territory 'vastness'; he strayed away from his residence 'beauty'. The time was when it was getting dark. The duration was (that of) a pig, the sun a snake and the stars birds. The person's designation became a half-blind old woman. The ancestry was of uncertain nature. Four persons aided the old woman. Then five savages turned up. Then came a person who backed them up. Then came a female thief. There was a single individual in whom all this was accumulated. Then there was a countless army gathering. Since that about which he became mistaken and strayed away from started from that which did not exist as such, it became a probability. The concrete forms of sentient beings exceed imagination. The ways of becoming lost and the intent to do so are as many as one can think of.[32]

This allegory, like most allegories, would remain quite enigmatic if it were not for Klong-chen rab-'byams-pa's elucidation of the key terms. He says:

> 'rDo-rje sems-dpa' is 'pure awareness' (*rig-pa*). The territory 'vastness' is the primordial ground. The residence 'beauty' is the self-manifestation of the ground (with) the gates of its spontaneous givenness. The time 'when it was getting dark' means that something presented itself that was to become the starting-point of losing itself because, in not recognizing itself for what it was, it seemed to be something other. The 'pig' duration is the period in which the loss of pure awareness (*ma-rig-pa*) proliferates into conceptual constructs. The 'snake' sun is the glaring aspect of conceptuality that takes the object-presentation to be something concrete. The 'bird' stars are the desires that lead to an involvement with and craving for objects.[33] The 'old woman' is the cognitive capacity that has become loss of pure awareness and now holds to the mistaken presentation. The 'uncertain ancestry' means becoming lost and confused because the self-presentation of the ground that comes in any guise is the common ground for straying far and becoming lost. The 'four persons' who aid (the old woman) are the four co-determinants. The 'five savages' are the five poisons. The one 'person who backs up all these' is the discursive mind. The one 'female thief' is irritation. The one 'person in whom all this is accumulated' is the unitary character of the presence of the state of being lost. Moreover, it is subjectivism that upholds and holds to this state of being lost. The 'army gathering' means that from this state there arise the many emotions. Since this 'becoming lost' has started from what has been 'initially pure' in such a way that it cannot even be said to have been something, it is termed a 'probability' because of the simultaneity (with the 'initially pure').[34]

Even so, there are still some points that need clarification. As has been pointed out before, it is merely to satisfy the analytical habits of ordinary thinking that a distinction is made between 'ground' or 'Being' (*gzhi*) and 'the ground's (or Being's) self-manifestation or self-presentation' (*gzhi-snang*) to itself as experiencer already embedded in this totality. The relationship between these two is similar to 'rest energy' as inward movement and its becoming outwardly visible 'radiation'. This 'outward radiation' is, to use analogical language, an information to be processed, and processing of the information involves selection, discrimination, in brief, 'intelligence' which decides whether what is at hand is to be 'radiation' or 'matter'. Since cognitiveness is part and parcel of the process, the resultant of this selection and decision is not, from the viewpoint of experience, one between body and mind, but the very body-mind complex or the status of a sentient being. The contrast between body and mind is a secondary abstraction and a further misplaced concretization. As Klong-chen rab-'byams-pa puts it:

> Although the primordial ground has nothing to do with any going astray, it is when the ground's self-manifestation occurs that the cognitive property not recognizing this process and itself for what it is, being as yet undecided but having already all the markings of becoming 'loss of pure awareness', disrupts the ground's self-manifestation and goes astray into the status of sentient being.[35]

It hardly needs to be pointed out that here again the emphasis is on process, and, consequently, the single term 'loss of pure awareness' (*ma-rig-pa*) covers a wider area and raises more problems than seems to be the case at first glance. Moreover, the whole process must be seen within the context of experience which as a dynamic configurative process comes as a distinct posturing which is indicated by such terms as 'upward-directedly free' and 'downward-directedly lost',[36] and what is implied by these terms is that meaning emerges both in a pre-reflective (as yet untrammeled by and free of thematic postulates) and a reflective manner (with thematic considerations gaining the upper hand). It is this latter aspect that is felt as much as it is known to be a loss, and since it still occurs within experience it is appropriately termed a 'cognate (emergent, co-existent) loss of pure awareness' (*lhan-cig-skyes-pa'i ma-rig-pa*), which quickly and imperceptively enters a phase of a growing specification of the configurative thematic contents of the experience characterized by a proliferation of concepts, aptly called a 'proliferatingly fragmenting loss of pure awareness' (*kun-tu brtags-pa'i ma-rig-pa*). If, in addition to these two kinds, the dynamic of the ground as it is in the process of manifesting itself is counted as a kind of loss of pure awareness, there is the third kind termed 'solipsistic loss of pure awareness' (*bdag-nyid gcig-pa'i ma-rig-pa*). Together, these three kinds constitute the dynamic causation of an emergent reality shorn of an obsolete static necessitarian form.[37]

One other point that must be underscored is that the apparent contrast between 'pure awareness' (*rig-pa*) and 'loss of pure awareness' (*ma-rig-pa*) is by no means a juxtaposition of separable entities; they are the continuum that is otherwise designated as the 'ground's self-manifestation' and a movement proceeding within experience.[38] In other words, 'loss of pure awareness' remains an awareness of or about a reflected content which constitutes its thematic focus. This is to say, where the potentiality for various meanings exists within a dynamic complex, such as referred to by the term 'ground' ('Being') or, emphasizing the dynamic character more succinctly, by 'the ground's ('Being's') self-manifestation as a spontaneous givenness', it is the inherent selective (cognitive) capacity or property (a predication which re-emphasizes the fact that there is no process that is value-free) within the dynamic complex which will determine which of the various possibilities will be realized, whether they be on the side of increased meaning or on the side of a progressive loss which, nevertheless, may yet act as a positive feedback in the over-all development.

It is for this reason that 'loss of pure awareness' is dealt with so extensively. It is that factor which sets up and represents a process of causation which, aided by co-determinants, is moving in a certain direction. These co-determinants also operate within the process and give it its configurative character. It is important to bear this character in mind because an experience is never a juxtaposition of discrete elements, rather its constituents interlace and form an organic unity. Nevertheless, any and each constituent of an experience can be made thematic as a specific topic which, seen within the dynamic process of the experience, is a co-determinant of it. Traditionally, four such co-determinants have been enumerated. There is, first of all, the co-determinant of the process itself which in its ongoing fluidity is the triple modality of 'loss of pure awareness'. Inseparable from and, as it were, crystallizing within the process itself, is the phenomenal field which, as a co-determinant, is both perceptual and valuational and thus determines 'what' the experience is to be. But this 'what' is inseparable from the 'who', the subject ready to accept the stimulation by the 'what' and in this readiness co-determining the configurative situation. Both the 'what' and the 'who' are tendencies, rather than solidified entities, within the total configuration. Lastly, there is the temporal horizon which encompasses, but does not arrange in a linear succession, the above-mentioned co-determinants, and is itself one of the co-determinants of an experience.[39]

The *Mu-tig 'phreng-ba* contains the remarkable and often quoted statement that

> Although that about which (the experiential process)
>   becomes mistaken and from which it strays away, is said
>   to have many facets,
> (Basically) it is the spontaneous givenness (of Being) and its
>   responsiveness.[40]

It will be remembered that the spontaneous givenness is the incipient 'outward' radiation of what is termed 'the initially pure' (facticity of Being) and that this givenness is responded to. The response is an interaction between the givenness and the responsiveness of Being. In this interaction, figuratively speaking, a state of tension is set up, which has both 'positive' and 'negative' charges, each of them being the center or source of a field. Again, with reference to lived-through experience, the first fact to note is the presence of two kinds of cognitiveness, and any experience situation or process can be charged with either one or the other kind. We have already encountered these two kinds: pristine cognitiveness (*ye-shes*) as the distinctly operative manifestation of the cognitive property of Being which, broadly speaking, is what we term pure awareness (*rig-pa*) or the 'positive' charge, and loss of pure awareness (*ma-rig-pa*), the 'negative' charge. Pursuing the analogy with electricity a little further, careful investigation shows that the 'positive' charge, 'pure awareness', stays with the 'ground' and seems (like the ground from which it is inseparable) to be immovable, and that it is the 'negative' charge, 'loss of pure awareness' that travels into what is termed Saṃsāra or 'negativity' that has no grounding whatsoever. Yet this 'negativity' acts like a test charge by which the 'positive' tension can be qualitatively measured. Such qualitative measurement is connected with 'intelligence' and with meanings which are values that are appreciated by intelligence, hence the attraction of the 'positive' charge A, exerting a force on the 'negative' charge B by which B is pushed towards A. In the same way, of course, the 'positive' A is pushed towards the 'negative' B by the field of B. This is what is meant by the statement of the process becoming mistaken about itself and straying away from its positive character. On the other hand, the 'positive' A is always exerting its force on B as the 'thrust towards Being'. Both the 'positive' and the 'negative' belong to the phase of the self-manifestation of Being, comparable in its radiation to electromagnetic energy. The 'radiation energy' presupposes 'pure energy' or Being-as-such and is indicated by such terms as 'initially pure', 'ground', 'open'.

It is in the *Rig-pa rang-shar chen-po'i rgyud* that we find a
discussion of the mutual attraction between 'negativity' and
'positivity' and the resolution of this oscillation in Being,
which continues without ever allowing itself to be reduced to
a being and which, without showing itself as a meaning, lets
things, that is, meanings appear:

> Listen, you who are of a pure nature in the center of Being.
> Understand the extent of the Buddha intentionality by the
> following:
> Once upon a time there lived in the country 'Vastness' a
> teacher, 'Light Diffusion' by name. He had two children who
> were captured in a lonely gorge. Then came five soldiers who
> overpowered them with their pointed spears. The two chil-
> dren were put into a dungeon, and a half-blind old woman
> locked the door. Then four servants came along and the five
> soldier-riders were taken from their horses. After the two
> children had recovered, they killed the prison guards; then they
> ran to (the castle) Sunlight and collected taxes. Having been
> counselled by twenty-one court-ladies, they resided in a
> magnificent palace. Their five champions donned their armor
> and guarded the gates. Nobody could enter the palace. Then,
> looking into four mirrors, the children recognized their own
> real nature. They saw the one mansion to have eight gates
> and they broke out into laughter about themselves.[41]

This terse allegorical story is elucidated by Klong-chen
rab-'byams-pa as follows:

> The teacher 'Light Diffusion' is self-existing pristine cognitive-
> ness. The two children are the initially pure cognitive property
> of Being and the pristine cognitiveness as it operates in the
> spontaneous givenness of Being. To be captured in a gorge
> means that, as to the presence of the spontaneous given-
> ness of Being, pristine cognitiveness is mistakenly differen-
> tiated into mother and child and fettered into Saṃsāra by
> the loss of pure awareness. To be overcome by five persons
> with pointed spears means that, when the five poisons have
> dislodged the cognitive property from its level, it is set

on the path of straying away (from its place into a 'dim' realm). To be locked up by an old woman means that, once the cognitive property has been locked by the loss of pure awareness, no escape is granted. To be seized by four servants and to have five persons deprived of their horses means that four (kinds of) appreciative discrimination purify the dividedness (engendered by) the five emotions together with the driving force behind this dividedness. The four appreciative discriminations are the 'one which sets free' and which releases from the emotions, the 'one which gathers' and which assembles the pristine cognitions, the 'one which discerns' and which separates the emotions from pristine cognitions, and the 'one which pushes on' and which moves the pristine cognitions on to the continuum of Being. The two children having recovered and killed the prison guards means that when the cognitive property of Being recognizes itself as what it is, karmic actions and the emotions-engendered dividedness, which have dimmed or fettered the property, are loosened and disappear without any trace. The two children hurrying to Sunlight and collecting taxes means that when the cognitive property has settled in the eyes[42] and looks at the presentation of the continuum and its pure awareness, the five senses are overpowered by this splendor and various felt experiences gather in this self-rising. To have been counselled by the court-ladies[43] and to have hurried to the palace guarded by five men carrying their shields means that when the pristine cognitions deriving from the cognitive property of Being have been pointed out by twenty-one encounters (with Being), it is by contemplating the self-manifestation (of Being) that the cessation of the oscillating movement of dividing thoughts comes from within, and a creatively illumining programming in a cluster of five light values comes from the steadiness that now reigns and that cannot be upset by dividing thoughts. To recognize that by looking at the pristine cognitions (mediated through) four lamps means that the meaning and value of the cognitive property residing in its place dawns within one's self. To start laughing when seeing the mansion to have eight gates means that by seeing the self-presentation of Being in its spontaneous givenness one has firmly taken one's seat in the continuum of Being that has been from a beginning without a beginning.[44]

As the last sentence in this explanation of the allegory shows, it is in Being-as-such that freedom, the ultimate goal of all striving, is found, though not as some thing to be obtained, but already present in the dynamic of Being-becoming, providing to the experiencing 'intelligence' a glimpse of itself through its 'gates'. As process Being-becoming is at once temporalized and spatialized, or as Klong-chen rab-'byams-pa explains this presentation (-presence):

> At this time, there is upward-directed the presence(-presentation) of the initially pure, like a cloudless sky; frontward-directed there is the presence(-presentation) of sheer lucency, like a rainbow in the atmosphere; and downward-directed there comes the presence(-presentation) of the six kinds of sentient beings, like the reflection of the moon in water or a mirage. These three presences come at one and the same time.[45]

All that has been said so far, and illustrated by quotations from Klong-chen rab-'byams-pa's works, shows that Klong-chen rab-'byams-pa as a thinker, in the true sense of the word, sets out to experience the ground of all beings, Being itself. This is a marked shift from the habitual way of dealing with or thinking of 'reality' in terms of entities neatly arrayed into material and mental qualities, or in terms of objective and subjective poles with the rigid reductionism that attends these notions. Reductionism is patent in the very question put forward by habitual thinking: "What is the nature of that which is?" and in this formulation the 'that which is' reflects a world-picture in which the world—all that is—is conceived of as a totality of separable and discrete entities. This totality of entities includes both 'subject' and 'object' which are alike in their 'entitative' character. However, the selective viewpoint of 'objectivity', with its further reduction of 'that which is' to substance and essential and accidental predicates, or to ultimate 'facts' that are reducible to properties and relations, is as unsatisfactory and incapable of accounting for and elucidating experience as is the equally selective viewpoint of 'subjectivity', which not only retains the world-picture of the world as a totality of entities but even puts upon the lonely epistemological subject the burden of creating the entities which it is going to experience.

Experience is never a thing, be this an 'object' or a 'subject'. It is the merit of Nāgārjuna to have pointed this out in the opening stanza of his Madhyamakakārikā, which is made up of two kinds of denial:[46] (a) the denial that there exists any entity (*med-pa*) and (b) the denial that, if a certain something exists, it has a given property (*ma-yin-pa*). The first denial (a) comprises three pairs of contrasting entities which are of the nature of (i) event (or, more precisely, event-particle, to use a term coined by A. Whitehead)—origination and cessation, (ii) motion (or, more exactly, moving mass)—coming and going, and (iii) substance (particular existent)—materially filled eternity before the world began and the eternity of empty duration after the world is no more.

The second denial (b) comprises the predicates non-different and non-identical and deals with properties and not with any object which has these properties. Apart from its implications for the analysis of propositions, Nāgārjuna's statement effectively destroys any reductionism and opens the way for recognizing experience as an open-dimensional movement that in its lived-through passage becomes configurative. But, then, each constituent in the configuration can be made a topic for reflection and given a 'standing-in-itself' status. When this happens, the deeply ingrained tendency to move in the direction of reductionism reasserts itself and is even supported by the use of argumentation by which metaphysicians attempt to support their claims.[47] These claims may be deductively conclusive simply because, as in a formal logical system, one starts from a set of axioms which are accepted as true, and then moves to a conclusion which must be the case and which also is the case as long as the (pre-established, in other words, arbitrarily postulated) axioms are accepted.

There is another type of metaphysics which is more tentative in its conclusions and involves a rather intricate analysis of such concepts as perception, cognition, illusion, as it primarily works with visual experiences, and in which the conclusion that the world may be 'like a dream', 'like an apparition', 'like an illusion' is validated by the facts of visual experience. There is a significant difference between such 'empirical' metaphysics and the rigid system of deductive metaphysics, between whether I say that the world is *like* an illusion or that it *is* an illusion.[48]

Traditionally eight images have been used to illustrate the tentative and suggestive character of what we uncritically accept as our 'world', and superficially it seems as if Klong-chen rab-'byams-pa relates these images to Nāgārjuna's negations. Actually, Klong-chen rab-'byams-pa goes far beyond Nāgārjuna and the limitations of empirical metaphysics. It is true, he uses the words and 'meanings' as they have already been uttered and have found a place in the language and cultural milieu of the speaker, but he also uses them to raise new points of view and fresh meanings and so these 'already available' words become organizing notions whose exact meanings emerge in the actualization of experience.[49] These notions are fluid, never fixed, and their validity lies in their ability to elucidate the actual context of man's life in a world which can never be sectioned into an interior or subjective sphere, on the one side, and an exterior or objective sphere, on the other. That which is intended by dreaming, to give the first example in Klong-chen rab-'byams-pa's dissertation, is not an object; neither is it a mere interiority. Dreaming is the experience of being-in-a-state in which solicitations and responses are reciprocal in establishing a configurative experience.

This fluidity of organizing notions is even more conspicuous in what is termed *sgyu-ma*, which can roughly be translated by 'magic' or 'wizardry' because of its compelling power to enchant and to astonish, but which defies any precision unless seen in the context in which its meaning emerges within experience. The meaning of 'magic' is different for the understanding of a situation in which one feels oneself enchanted, ensnared, trapped, and where the presentative solicitation by enchantment is responded to by 'counter-magic', than it is for the understanding of a situation in which one wonders and marvels at the extraordinariness, perfection, beauty, and even inexplicableness of what is presented and responded to in sheer wonderment and appreciation.

Klong-chen rab-'byams-pa himself brings out this fluid and open-ended character of organizing notions in his explanation of the title of the dissertation:

> *sgyu-ma* ('wizardry') is something that has no truth in itself. It is twofold: In its impure form it is the enchantment in Saṃsāra, like being a tired traveller; in its pure form it is the wonderment at Nirvāṇa, experienced as a comfortable lodging-place, the truth that is sheer lucency, the continuum that is Being, as is stated in the *gSang-snying*:[50]
> The real in two forms of wizardry.
> 'Finding comfort and ease' (*ngal-gso*) means that the mind can rest cozily in this comfortable lodging-place which, ultimately, is the initially pure fact of Being and, for the time being, the meaningfulness of Being defying any propositions about it.[51]

CHAPTER ONE

Dreaming[1]

There is growing evidence that the world is 'not just out there' to be looked at by a detached spectator, but that the spectator is so deeply involved in his field of observation that at every moment he is a participant in what is going on. This involves a shift from objects to events, and from substance to process—from a mechanistic world view to a dynamic web of interacting processes. As a participant man is no longer a distinct entity, but is inseparably linked to his 'world', whose structure he determines, while at the same time he is influenced and molded by this world. Man's solidity, his very identity, is dissolved and becomes protean, dream-like, a presence that is and has nothing about which it could be said that this is it. Yet a presence is that which is presented, which appears and is placed within the focus of attention occurring in a spatio-temporal horizon. As a presentation any presence solicits a response which becomes a lived-through experience. The response, in a certain sense, adds to the paradox of 'presence'-presentation. Man, a process himself, now attempts to report on what has been, and still is, going on. He simultaneously participates in his dream-world by dreaming, and reports on it by creating the illusion of 'reality' which holds him spell-bound. It is the process of dreaming, rather than the dream itself, that symbolizes and conjures up before our eyes what we are, what we need, and what we pretend to be in order to be. Dreaming takes place spontaneously, producing and enacting self-contained presentations which become mistaken concretizations of the very process that is going on, and which become progressively estranged from their underlying rhythms.

The spontaneity of the dream process carries with it the convincing quality of being a possibility for feeling and for imagining, above all because it is not 'of this world' which exhibits a structure in which everything can be deduced or inferred from conceptual schemata that have been 'born', come into this world, and as such are rigidly circumscribed, mutually exclusive and distinctly separable. Being 'unborn' and irreducible to an event-particle, termed 'origination', spontaneity points to and even is an infinite dynamic field out of which everything 'not existing prior to its being born' (created, made manifest) is in the process of 'appearing', 'presenting itself', indeed, making its presence both felt and known. Everything becomes present as *its* own 'presentation' which has both novelty and a dynamic cohesion with anterior phases. Without this double character the 'presentness' of a particular presentation would be irremediably destroyed. This continued becoming also accounts for the uncertainty of what is going to happen. As long as any event is not yet present (is as yet 'unborn'), its specific character remains uncertain because it is only its presentness which establishes its specificity, thereby ending its uncertainty through its concrete realization of itself.

In the specific example of a dream, its 'presence'-presentation is like the 'creation' of a photon in the act of its own emission, and its spontaneity is the totality of itself, that is, of Being. This is to say that what, to the analytic habit of ordinary thinking, appears as two realms, staticness of 'things' (Being) and dynamics of 'motion' (presentation, spontaneity), is inseparably fused into a single dynamic notion which, as experience, antedates its dissection into these two realms. This, in the language of poetic imagination, is sheer 'wizardry' (*sgyu-ma*)—in the more technical language of philosophy which, under favorable circumstances, may still preserve something of the felt imagery or of imaged feeling that characterizes genuine experience, it is both 'open' (*stong-pa*) and 'lucent', 'radiant' (*gsal-ba*). Wizardry, by its very openness which in everyday language is just nothing, allows the emergence of structure that becomes progressively more differentiated; by its very lucency, it provides an opening up and a marking out of spatio-temporal universes. Openness and radiance are inseparable in determining the structure of the 'cloudlike' condensations of a 'field' or continuum likened to the vast expanse of the sky. These condensations are not independent entities but transient manifestations of this dynamic field in the manner of local perturbations which under suitable circumstances may disappear again. Openness and radiance belong to the domain of experience without which they themselves would lose all meaning, as a dynamic process experience is imbued with and becomes structured by intentionality. This very dynamic is tendential (*rig-pa*) in that it exhibits certain tendencies and dispositions to relate and to arrange the content of experience as meant. These meanings are not imposed 'from the outside' but develop in the ongoing process of experience. The most important point to note is that none of the aspects termed 'open', 'radiant', 'tendential' can ever be seen as isolated entities—they can only be understood in terms of their interrelated activity.

The indivisibility of 'openness' and 'radiance' may be illustrated by referring to a distinction between two kinds of energy, well known in modern physics. On the basis of this distinction 'openness' would represent the 'energy of inward movement'. But since 'inward' and 'outward' are relational in meaning, they are to be thought of as two different but related aspects of a single process of movement. 'Openness' may further be said to represent and, as an inward movement, have 'rest energy' (E_0) and rest mass (m_0): $m_0 = E_0 c_2$.[2] Because of the ongoing 'inward movement', which may be called 'primary mobility',[3] being capable, because of this nature, of undergoing transformations into other forms of energy whose effect will be 'outward' movement, the 'rest energy' and, with it, the 'rest mass' will undergo a corresponding decrease. If 'rest mass' ('openness') is inward movement, then something without rest mass must be wholly 'outward' movement ('radiance') and as pure outward movement ('sheer lucency') it is as yet uncompromised as to any particular frame of reference. As such, it is also 'pure intentionality', 'pure awareness', 'purely tendential' (*rig-pa*).

By this additional 'qualification' the observer-turned-participant is inseparably included in the total process without necessitating the assumption of a timeless ego or an eternal essence. Intentionality imbues and structures experience, which is that which is lived through in distinct frames of reference. Through these frames of reference that which is taking place becomes a topic of attention. Every occasion of experience exhibits tendencies and, with them, dispositions which map out the direction into which experience may move, and which particular configurations it may assume. The consequence is that 'radiance', which, as we have seen, is as yet uncompromised in one frame of reference, will be different, in another frame of reference, with regards to its direction of movement and its 'light frequency'. This new frame of reference constitutes the appropriation of the content of the experience as content for the experiencer finding himself within a certain situation. In other words, 'pure intentionality' (*rig-pa*) becomes 'vested intentionality', loss of pure awareness (*ma-rig-pa*) which is coextensive and co-emergent (*lhan-cig-skyes-pa*) with the changed frame of reference. Once such a new frame of reference becomes established, which may be likened to a movement at speed less than light ('radiance'), such movement, if uniform, can always be transformed into rest or a velocity equal to that of what is going to be under consideration.

In terms of Mind, this new phase or movement is the emergence of *a* mind as a noetic-noematic complex with an ever increasing recrudescence of itself and its correlated contents, and with a marked insistence on the distinction between 'internal' and 'external', that is, interiority of subject and exteriority of object. This change-over from 'pure intentionality' to 'vested intentionality' with its characteristic subject-object dichotomy is itself a complex process in which conceptual, volitional, and emotional tendencies intermingle, interpenetrate and as reciprocal movements vitalize, organize and color each other so that a contextually differentiated horizon of representational meanings is conjured up, from which it is nevertheless possible to work one's way back to the experiential source from which the subject-object dichotomy has sprung. However, the coerciveness of this 'vested intentionality', pervading every aspect of its ensuing subject-object diversification, is felt as having a bewitching effect that lures us into a realm which breaks down the very moment we try to hold it. For this reason, this phase of experience, creating and enjoying its own presentations and their variation, is termed 'wizardry of wrong notions'.

As in the case of 'openness' and 'radiance', it is evident that the evocative terms 'wizardry of pure Being' and 'wizardry of wrong notions' are inherently relational in meaning. Thus, relative to the 'outward' wizardry of wrong notions and the increasingly fictitious mapping of the experienced world, the dynamic of pure Being is 'inward' and more 'to the point' of what is going on. Relative to the 'inward' wizardry of pure Being, the spatio-temporal displacement into dichotomic representations and their *ad hoc* explanations is 'outward'. They are held together in experience, of which both are interpretations, so that in the 'wizardry of wrong notions' there is always something disquietingly present from the 'wizardry of pure Being' and in the 'wizardry of pure Being' there is imagery borrowed from the 'concreteness' of 'wrong notions'.

The analogy of dreaming is a clear rejection of a view which regards the world as a totality of entities neatly separated into material and mental varieties; instead it points to the 'self-emerging' or self-presentation of a process of experiencing which comes *before* its decomposition into objectifiable entities. Man's 'world' has, like a dream, no substantive reference, but indicates a texture of experience in which intentionality points to possible perspectives. Perspective issues from and is of something, and this reinstates the experiencer inside the process. In no way is there an ego (transcendental or pure) involved, rather it is human existence as the ongoing process of experiencing—dream-like—that functions as the ground of interpretative and ongoing notions. A lived–through experience is a process structured by its very intentionality. The shift from thing (substance) to process (movement), and from the postulate of subject and object to lived-through experience, introduces a new approach to the meaning of being, traditionally termed ontology. Being becomes presentation, presence, which involves its experiencing (experience). But from where has being (experience-experiencing-experienced-world) 'appeared' and presented itself? The answer cannot but be 'from nowhere' and the consequence is that its spontaneous presence-presentation 'exists' only for a relatively brief time and thereafter leaves no trace behind. In the harsh and unfeeling terms of science this is a vacuum fluctuation; in terms of lived-through experience it is dreaming.

Praise to Śrī Vajrasattva[4]

A   **O**ut of the dynamic reach and range[5] where all that
can be is (still) alike in (not yet) having originated,
There emerges the majestic play of the
wonderment of pristine cognition beyond any
duality, (which reigns as)
A self-existing primordiality, Mind-as-such, the King—
Him I salute by virtue of the fact that there has been no
origination into separate entities and that (all that is
is such that nothing) can be added to or subtracted
from it.[6]

B   In order to understand what is meant by the
pronouncement
Of the Victorious One that all that is partakes of two
varieties of wizardry,
I have collated the very essence of the Sūtras, Tantras,
Upadeśas.[7]
Listen to my explication of how I have experienced it.

CIa   Out of the dynamic reach and range of openness and
lucency, defying all attempts to capture it in
propositions,
(Similar to) the vast expanse of the sky, Mind-as-such,
the unchanging continuum that is the Ground
(or Being),[8]
There are manifested, like the sun and the moon and
the stars, the flawless Buddhahood constituents,
(Being's) spontaneity, the indivisible unity of three
founding strata and their (founded) pristine
cognitions,

In themselves a sheer lucency, yet with all capabilities[9]
    complete:
This is the primordial presence of Being in its actuality
    (given in and through experience).
It is termed 'pure wizardry of Being'.

From out and over this very reach and range there move   CIbi
    clouds that have arisen at random and wander about
    aimlessly,
In the manner of sleep, the creator of dreams.
(This is Being's) cognate (and coextensive) loss of
    intrinsic awareness[10] (by which it fails to know itself
    as it really is).
(In the wake of this loss there arises) the mind deceived
    by its assuming a duality where there is none,
    (leading to)
A proliferating decrease in intrinsic awareness.[11] Due to
    these (two losses)
The variety of the mistaken presentations (by Being to
    itself), exemplified in the forms of the six kinds of
    sentient beings, is like the process of dreaming.

This (paradox of a) presence without anything present   CIbii
    is individually experienced as either happiness or
    misery,
All of which is a process of habituation that has been
    going on for a long time (in the sense that)
One's status, physical existence, scope of enjoyment,
    and so on
Are the happiness or misery that derive from good and
    evil as a self-presentation (of Being in slanted
    perspectives),
In its varied shadings like a finished painting.
In becoming mistaken about itself, the one (Mind)
    presents itself to itself in many (guises),

And by taking the many guises as something real, its
   flow of mistaken presentations does not stop.
Alas! this actuality (of Being) presenting itself as
   fictitious being is like a dream.

CIbiii   This dream presence with its multiple and varied
            contents, (which is)
         The intellect moving in a subject-object division as
            regards the mistaken presentation in its sleep, which
            is the loss of intrinsic awareness concerning
         The facticity (of Being as) the one self-existing
            Mind-as-such,
         Does not exist as anything else and in anywhere else
            but this self-existing Mind-as-such.
         (This dream presence-)presentation the Victorious One
            has termed 'wizardry of wrong notions'.

CIbiv   Just as for a person who has swallowed the seeds of the
            thorn-apple
         Whatever appears in all its variety is but a
            hallucination,
         So also, for those who are intoxicated by the sleep
            that is the loss of intrinsic awareness,
         Whatever is there before the mind having
            become mistaken about itself, (in assuming itself to
            be one of) the six kinds of sentient beings,[12]
         Has no truth or reality value in itself. This very moment
            understand this!

CIbv   Since mistaken presentations are tied up with mistaken
            interferences and a (subsequent) proliferation into
            mistaken notions,
         The state in which there is neither truth nor falsity and
            which in its non-duality passes beyond the intellect
         Must, of a certainty, be known to be the self-existent
            intrinsic awareness.

In its vastness which is unbound by the boundaries (set
    by such predications as) not being this and not
    existing as this,
Know Buddha intentionality to be like the (expanse of
    the) sky.

The actuality of all that is is like a dream.   CIc
From that time onward when it made its presence felt, it
    has had nothing substantial about it, and
While in its incessant presentation, in which its
    observable qualities are not obliterated,
It is for the short time (of its presence) false, but if its
    observable qualities being the concretizations of an
    open dimension
Are properly investigated, it turns out to be neither true
    nor false,
Neither existing nor non-existing, in its actuality
    passing beyond (these conceptual) limitations.
Like the sky, beyond words and unencumbered by
    objects of thought,
Know this actuality to have been pure (and clear) from
    its beginningless beginning.

The instruction as to how to experience directly (this
    dream-like character) through the exercise of
    creative imagination—once it
Has been ascertained by direct vision[13] that all that is,
The world of appearances and the fictions about it,
    Saṃsāra and Nirvāṇa, is similar to a dream—is as
    follows:
Sit cross-legged on a comfortable seat, and then
Take refuge and activate the ethical impulse;[14]
And then call up this wizardry (of Being) presenting
    itself (to itself)
Out of its open reach and range where all that can be is
    alike and complete (in being an open possibility).[15]

CIIaii When you clearly envisage the Gurus of your tradition
in such a manner that they are indivisible from
The basic Guru,[16] surrounded by the host of tutelary
deities and Ḍāka-Ḍākinīs
In the very center on a (throne built by) sun and moon
and lotus, in your head,
You make offerings to them, praise them and pray to be
enabled to deal competently with the dream
(process),
And you must imagine
Yourself and the world of appearances together with
the fictions about it to dissolve in a pure light and
then to fade away in the Guru,
And then for a while to stay relaxed in this reach and
range that is like the sky.
Thereby graced, a deep understanding comes by itself.

CIIbi Afterwards, the manner in which to imagine creatively
what actually is involved is
Again and again to imagine creatively that,
In the external objective world, mountains, valleys,
countries, as well as
Earth, water, fire, space, sentient beings and so on,
The five objects of color, sound, fragrance, flavor,
touch,
And, in the internal subjective world, (your) body,
sensory perceptions and all (their) meanings are just
a dream.

CIIbii All that has happened up to yesterday's (events)
Is similar to last night's dream, a content of
(subjective) mind.
Even what is present now is but your intellect's activity,
nothing as such and yet being there.
Yesterday and today are like a dream and
Tomorrow and day after tomorrow are a dream not
yet come.

Having firmly set up the idea that all that presents itself
     to you, for negation and affirmation and
As happiness and misery, is a dream,
Do not for a moment harbor the idea that there is a
     true mind.

With unwavering attention hold (the idea) that   CIIbiii
     (everything is) like a dream
Regardless of whether you are walking, sitting, eating,
     moving about or conversing.
When you are not separate from the idea that
Whatever is present, whatever is being done, and
     whatever is thought about is all a dream,
Then you train yourself in absolute non-subjectivity
     (by realizing that your dream)
Has no truth-value, is but something flimsy, something
     ethereal, something evanescent,
Something fleeting, something faint.

When you have (through your investigation)   CIIbiva
     understood that the mistaken presentation
     (concretized into) an object to be dealt with is just
     a dream,
The release from (the coerciveness of) this noematic
     aspect of mind automatically leads to the release
     from (the coerciveness of) its noetic aspect:
Where there is no object there is no subject.

Sometimes when you have looked outwards, inwards,   CIIbivb
     and in-between for the mind
That encounters what appears (before it) as a dream,
This intellectual activity, that has nothing before it that
     it can grasp concretely,
Is just this reach and range that is similar to the sky
     extending into all directions.

This intrinsic awareness divorced from the frantic
   searching that goes with the intentiveness of
   attention (to particulars),
Comes by itself as an openness and lucency defying
   any propositions.
When there is no 'grasping' there is nothing 'grasped'.
When there is freedom from 'grasping' objects because
   the subject (that does the grasping) has been left
   behind,
There is no connection with an object (into which the
   presence is turned), and the confines of
   investigation appear to dissolve.
At this time (what is there) is the non-dual, self-existent
   pristine cognitiveness.

CIIbv   When you have understood it thus and have become
   familiar with it,
Then you are free from the addiction to (the duality of)
   object and mind because the noematic and the
   noetic have been left behind.
After having had this experience in which what is
   present is not held to be this or that,
Whatever presents itself arises in primal openness[17]
   having no root whatsoever.
This is the experience of Being in its actual
   primordiality.

CIIbvia   When gradually the concretization of the (aesthetic)
   presence into an object, the 'impure' enchantment,
Dissolves in the 'pure' enchantment, and once the
   objectifying interference with (the 'aesthetic'
   presence) as this or that has been left behind, that
   which comes into the foreground
Is the growing into limpid clearness and consummate
   perspicacity in the primal ground.

This is like the awakening from sleep when the
  mistaken presentations of dreaming are no more.

This (process of Mind) becoming mistaken about itself   CIIbvib
  and going astray has not existed previously (as
  something) nor does it exist later (as something) but
  is present here and now.
But although being a presence, it is not experienced as
  something existing ever since it has made its
  presence felt.
Since the intellectual activity, being led astray by
  inveterate tendencies, while being nothing and yet
  being there,
In its actuality has been pure since its beginningless
  beginning, it is similar to a dream.

In the same way as that which presents itself internally   CIIbvic
  as a dream
Does not so exist before one falls asleep nor after one
  awakens from it,
But is there at the time of sleep and even then is
  nothing specific in itself,
So also know this paradox of a presence without
  anything present to have neither foundation
  nor root.

When you make yourself familiar (with this dream-like   CIIci
  character of 'reality') during daytime,
And now at night are about to be engulfed by sleep,
You must lie down on your right side on a
  comfortable bed,
In the posture of the Buddha passing into Nirvāṇa,
  and when
The motility (in the body) becomes hardly noticeable
  and the eye movements cease (to be erratic)—
You must fix your mind on the point in the heart, where

from the white-colored short sound-syllable A
(like a) crystal globe a pure light shines forth,
Becoming subtler and subtler (by decreasing in size)
from a finger's breadth (to the tip of a hair),
And you must not allow the dream-like attention to it
to swerve.
Thereby a dream-like sheer lucency arises.

CIIcii   At first you may have terrifying dreams
But by attending to them as dreams their terrifying
features disappear by themselves.
To have a holistic experience within this reach and
range of dreaming
Is to have captured dreaming. This the practitioner
should know.

CIIciii   Afterwards you have to practice[18] dreaming as having
absolutely nothing real about itself;
Moreover, the intellectual activity that goes astray in
this paradox of a presence without anything present
Is similar to a dream; it cannot be grasped concretely;
Know it to be beyond the intellect moving in categories
of true and false.

CIIciv   Afterwards, even when it comes to the creation and
transformation (of imaginative realities)
While imagining (yourself) as recasting yourself into
any shape you desire,
Be this a god of the Brahmā world,
A Buddha or a Bodhisattva and so on,
You must at this period of dreaming let (this activity) go
on in the reach and range that has nothing real
about itself.

CIIcv   Afterwards, at every instant,
Whether you transform yourself from a god of the

Brahmā world into Indra, or from a god into man,[19]
as you like,
You have to imagine this to take place in the reach and
range that has nothing real about itself.

Afterwards you must exercise this creative ability to   CIIcvi
counteract (the phenomena) as a means to train
(beings) by
Multiplying (yourself) into a hundred thousand and ten
million (replicas).

Afterwards you may go wherever you want, be it   CIIcvii
To the pure realm or to (distant) regions of the world or
to 'Og-min,[20]
And you may see the Buddhas and listen to their
flawless message.
Holistic experiences through pristine cognitions and
clouds of spiritual sustenance are realized.
When by day and night you have continuously
practiced and realized this through your intentive
attention,
What then comes about is the capabilities of intrinsic
awareness;
Not contradicting their very nature they are being
made manifest.
This is the most profound and essential spiritual
pursuit.

When thus by day and night you have dealt creatively   CIIIa
with dreaming
You are freed from the tether that holds you to (the
notions of) substance and quality.
Fences, mountains, and walls offer no obstacles
And higher forms of cognition and countless holistic
experiences are lived through.
A superior pristine cognitiveness that is unlimited in its
felt value and understanding is born.

CIIIb Ultimately, when you have reached the primordial
continuum (of experience) that is Mind-as-such,
The bitendential value of Being[21] is spontaneously, as
in a dream, realized:
The value that Being has for you in itself—(you yourself
being) an (ultimate) founding stratum of
meaning—and the value that Being represents to
others—(you yourself being) the two founding strata
of apprehendable (and appreciable) meanings.
Therefore, creatively attend to this process that is like
a dream.

CHAPTER TWO

Wizardry—Enchantment—
Wonderment[1]

That which we call our 'reality' turns out, on closer
inspection, to be our intended meanings (*chos*), which
present themselves like a dream from nowhere and out
of nothing, which yet reaches into our alleged reality without
ever being or becoming something, for in order to be something it ought first to have come into 'existence', which
functions as the source of interpretative notions. But if our
reality comes from nowhere and out of nothing and, therefore, shares in these 'qualities' of nowhere and nothing, we
cannot say anything pertinent or valid about it, because
then nowhere would already be somewhere, and nothing,
something. Consequently whatever we may say about our
'reality' is 'untrue'; it is merely a fiction, veridical only in its
approximation to the fictional scheme which we have developed as our 'reality' and into which we have unwittingly
allowed ourselves to be drawn. Whichever way we may turn
we find ourselves in a paradoxical situation: nothing is yet a
being-there, a presence and presentation. This can only
mean that nothing is a dynamic nothing, not a static or

mechanical nothing (*bem-stong*); it is an utter 'openness' that determines the diaphanous and radiant character of thereness. This thereness is a dynamic process, and not only does it solicit responses but it is also constantly responded to, and this interaction sets up interference patterns that eventually are interpreted, conceptually as well as valuationally, and then concretized into Saṃsāra and Nirvāṇa.

That 'nothing', in ordinary parlance, or the 'openness of Being', in the cumbersome language of philosophy, should present itself as a diaphanous and radiant presence, a being-there to be dealt with, is in its very act of presentation ('appearing') imbued with the atmosphere of miraculousness and dealt with by countering it by magic—magic in some sense being a response to a compelling force already acting upon us. This atmosphere of miraculousness has an inexorable character felt as sheer wizardry, valued for its wonderment and disvalued for being an enchantment, and is also known as being but an apparition. Miraculousness is a characteristic of lived-through experience, determining the multiple variations that occur in this process. A further exploration of experience reveals a dual character and movement. There is the 'wizardry' of the process of experience itself. This is certainly distinct from the 'magic' of explicating this process, but this explication still occurs within the process of experience without being a repetition of the experiential process. The analogies employed are means to explicate; they are not arguments for the existence of this process. If existence has any meaning for experience it is derivative, not primary or even prior to experience. The 'wizardry' of the experiential process and the 'magic' of its explications are interwoven and interrelated in such a manner that the experiencer is simultaneously in these two worlds.

More specifically, as a dynamic process, lived-through experience constitutes a tension field: the pull in one direction, Saṃsāra, a state of increasing quantification—one is almost tempted to speak of it as an entropy-seeking system—is countered by another in the direction of Nirvāṇa which is felt as a quality irreducible to quantity and hence closer to Being as total meaningfulness and valuableness. In this tension between opposing forces within one and the same field constituting a dynamic process, the process is 'aware' of or imbued with purpose and meaning and value. Purpose involves directionality which can easily be misunderstood as leading to an end state that is purely quantitative. However, against such a one-sided interpretation of directionality speaks the fact that purpose introduces and even is bound up with a valued, in other words, qualitative aspect. More specifically, quality relates to existence as experienced Being and, because of the overarching role of experience, it is noticeable in tonus $(khams)^2$ which expresses the vital energy in ourselves, tending towards an optimum performance level. As purpose or value this movement is termed 'thrust towards (well-)Being' which operates in each sentient, that is, experiencing being. In this thrust Being is guided towards itself by leaving behind the empty shell of an isolated self. This movement may not always enjoy actualization because of disruptive forces overshadowing this thrust, but it is always present as a task to be undertaken.

The oneness of Being and experiencing is such that Being, ever present in us as a task and open possibility—which has nothing to do with either the category of being in traditional philosophy or with the random derivation conceded in a universe of statistical determination—is revealed in the experience of its open dimension, and that experiencing, the unceasing dynamic of Being, directs our being towards its inherent freedom from which the process itself has started. Such oneness does away with any view that derives from, or tries to save, a static universe and, by implication, with any reductionism, the ultimate of quantification and exclusion of quality. Such oneness brings to light and focuses on the creativity of a living system such as man. It is from the viewpoint of lived-through experience, rather than from reflective rational cognition which is hardly ever interested in process, that this creativity is referred to as 'wizardry' issuing, as it were, from within the process itself. In this process man is not merely receptive and passively led into a state of enchantment by a welter of apparitions, but he responds actively in shaping a world of qualities transparent to meanings. In this mood we participate in life's flow, fully aware of its fascination, its incredible wealth of facets— not as detached and alienated spectators but as creative participants.

gain, the statement by the Victorious One that all that is, in its having nothing specific about[3] it, Is like the magic of an apparition, Is the very message of the Sūtras, Tantras, and Upadeśas. Listen to my explication of how I have experienced (this apparitional character of our reality).

In the same way as pristine cognitions (rise) spontaneously AIa
In Mind-as-such which is like the vast expanse of the sky in which the sun and the moon and the stars[4] (shine brightly),
So also out of the depth of the continuum of Being, infinite and wondrous (in its process of becoming),
The prolificness of concepts moving in the subject-object division (as the result of) the loss of pure awareness has come all by itself in such a way that
(Being) has presented itself in the mistaken identity of the six kinds of sentient beings ranging over the three world spheres, like an enchanting apparition.

(Being's presence) is self-presentational by the power of AIb
the interaction of causes and conditions
In the same way as the optical illusion of horses, elephants, men and women,
Mountains and palaces and so on appears out of
A combination of pieces of wood, pebbles, and magic spells.

AIc　The intellect which is a devious phenomenon of
　　　inveterate tendencies due to the loss of pure
　　　awareness
　　　Displays itself as an objective realm of presence and
　　　possibilities as well as a subjective realm, and the
　　　three poisons,[5] (accompany) the belief in the
　　　concreteness (of these realms).
　　　While actually there is nothing specific (in either), there
　　　is yet an unceasing presentation.
　　　This very moment unequivocally understand
　　　That all this (in its totality), resembling a magic show,
　　　Has no truth in it and is but open-dimensional imagery.

AIIa　All that is, (the world of) appearances and the
　　　possibilities it holds, Saṃsāra and Nirvāṇa,
　　　Has been, in what it really is, like the sky, remaining
　　　identical within itself.[6]
　　　Know it to have never come into existence and to have
　　　been pure from its beginningless beginning.

AIIb　This dynamic reach and range where the miracle occurs
　　　that what is without origin does originate
　　　Can be systematically presented by four illustrative
　　　instances of magic spell-weaving:
　　　(i) The actual wizardry that constitutes our being (as a
　　　task) to be solved;
　　　(ii) The enchantment that draws us into a deficiency
　　　state, the contamination that has to be got rid of;
　　　(iii) The counter-magic of instrumentality as an aid to
　　　remove contaminations; and
　　　(iv) The wonderment of pristine cognitions, as the goal
　　　where one has reached the end (of one's labors).

AIIbi　In the same way as in an optical illusion set up
　　　by spells,[7]

Chips and pebbles appearing as horses and elephants
Remain chips and pebbles and are not horses and
    elephants.
So also know the unreality of all that is and that which
    points out this unreality
As the actual wizardry (of Being) and its
    spell-weaving (in what is its presence).
The ground (or our being), that goes astray in becoming
    mistaken about itself, and the deterioration which
    takes place in this process are the course (Being
    takes) in losing (itself).
The presence of (Being's) mistaken identity and the
    freedom from (any) mistakenness are the features of
    (dynamic) freedom,[8] that has been since its
    beginningless beginning.
An orderly sequence of four phases marks the magic
    spell-weaving that illustrates (the internal wizardry
    of Being):
The illustrative material that is there before it is used
    for illustrative purposes; its application for specific
    illustration;
The finished illustration; and the initial state of affairs
    after the illustration has served its purpose.

The actual wizardry is Mind-as-such, a sheer lucency—   AIIbiia
It is the continuum that is there as our being that is to
    be restored to its originality; it is the thrust
    towards Being.

Not predetermined as either pure or impure,   AIIbiia
Beyond both Saṃsāra and Nirvāṇa,
This (lucency) is the foundation for what continues as
    Saṃsāra and Nirvāṇa,
(Each) coming from and representing pure awareness or
    its loss:
This (lucency) is primordial Being, experienced Being
    present as experience.

biia2
In the same way as the brightness of a mirror lets
     images appear in it,
But is not abolished by their appearances and
Remains the mirror surface, having nothing of
     blackness or whiteness in it,
Yet allows both blackness and whiteness to appear—
A person who knows Being's likeness with a mirror
     becomes wise in every respect.

IIbiib
Enchantment which draws us into a deficiency state is
     the mistaken presentation (of Being) as Saṃsāra;
It appears as this by having taken its nonduality as a
     duality.

IIbiic
The counter-magic of instrumentality is the path as an
     aid (for Being to recover itself):[9]
Through creative imagination that refines the two
     accumulations and the two stages
On the four phases of preparing, linking, seeing, and
     cultivating
It dispels the contaminations to be removed,
     like clouds.

Ibiid
The wonderment of pristine cognitions is the path of
     no-more-learning when one has come to the end of
     one's labors;
It is the spontaneous presence of the Victorious One's
     three founding strata and His charismatic activity.
It means that the fact of (our) having two purities[10] has
     come out into the open.

AIIc1
The magic spell-weaving illustrative (of Being's
     wizardry) is the magic of functional correlation:[11]
Like the images that have been conjured up by (the
     combination of) materials and spells.
Realize that all that is is just (such) unreality.
It comes from the weaving of a web of magical
     presentations.

In the same way as it is known that anything that appears as something other
Than the combination of materials and spells is a mistaken identity,
So also the presence mistaken to be sentient beings does not exist really (as these beings),
But must be known as only a presentation of functional correlation with all the vagaries of inveterate tendencies,
Having been nothing since it has been there and having nothing in it that could be grasped concretely,
Beyond the limitations of existence and non-existence.

AIIc2

The presence of the six kinds of sentient beings must be known in the same way as
The presence of make-believe countries and make-believe towns,
Make-believe persons and make-believe enjoyment,
Make-believe happiness and misery, make-believe origination and destruction,
Make-believe truth and falsehood.

AIIc3

Realize that the presence mistaken to be Saṃsāra is an enchanting apparition (for the following reasons):
Since it has been pure from its beginningless beginning it is not only like an enchanting apparition,
But since it is there while there is nothing, it is on the same level as an enchanting apparition;
Because it has come into existence under (favorable) conditions it resembles an enchanting apparition, and
As it is deceptive and perishable it is like an enchanting apparition.[12]

AIIc4

Since it has not been understood that the indubitable presence

AIIc5

Of the six kinds of sentient beings is but in the manner
of an apparition,
We have continuously lost ourselves in this city of
Saṃsāra with no boundaries.
How pitiable are those tormented by (their personal
feelings of) happiness and misery induced by
their actions![13]
You people, get it into your heads that this mistaken
identity (of Saṃsāra) is an enchanting apparition!

AIIc6 You who are fortunate (enough to see) should through
direct vision ascertain the fact that
The very meaning of all that is, not having originated
from anywhere nor going anywhere,
Nor residing anywhere, as well as
Its actual (presence as what there is), has been (the
wizardry of Being and is a presence as) an
apparition, pure since the beginningless beginning.

AIIIa You who are fortunate (enough to see) should know
this very moment that
The sentient beings are there like an enchanting
apparition, and
That the limpid clearness and consummate perspicacity
(that constitutes Buddhahood) is an enchanting
apparition, and that the dynamic reach and range
(of both)
Is the play of the wizardry (of Being) not admitting of
the duality of Saṃsāra and Nirvāṇa.

AIIIb1 According to the statement by the Victorious One that
not so much as an atom is observed
Apart from the enchantment by the apparitionalness of
all that is,
Those who desire liberation must know
That the fact that nothing whatsoever has any truth in it
is the very meaning of enchantment by
apparitionalness.

The ways of the wizardry (of Being) can also be known   AIIIb2
   in this way:
The wonderment of limpid clearness and consummate
   perspicacity is a spontaneity, never stepping out of
   itself nor changing into anything else,
Non-deceptive, an all-pervading authority, forever like
   the sky and
The sun or like a precious jewel fulfilling (mankind's)
   aspirations,
Displaying itself with perfect ease sportively in
   charismatic activities that have infinite qualities,
Pure and lucent, defying all propositions about it.

The enchantment which draws us into Saṃsāra is   AIIIb
   untrue and deceptive,
Having no connotative significance it is like an
   apparition, while there is nothing, there is yet a
   presence.
When the mistaken notions (about it) have been
   purified, the mistaken identity dissolves completely,
In the same manner as there is no longer a presence of
   horses and elephants when the spell has been
   broken.
(Similarly) a presence (which is reduced into a concrete)
   object (presenting) the contamination (that is
   Saṃsāra), the subject-object dichotomy, regains its
   freedom in (its) beginningless beginning;
Nothing as such in its purity, the presence has no
   ontological status.

The wizardry of Being is the very meaning of Being,   AIIIb4
   never stepping out of itself nor changing into
   anything else.
This meaningfulness of Being, that underlies all that is
   pure and impure,

Is like the empty space in a clay jar and a golden vase;
It neither increases nor decreases regardless of whether
    the vessel is intact or broken.
Similarly the very meaning of Being remains (the same),
    neither increasing nor decreasing, being neither
    good nor evil,
Regardless of the temporality of mistaken (bondage) or
    (inherent) freedom.
This is the real intentionality of Being in experienced
    Being.
If you know it in this way you are a wise person.[14]

BI   When you have gained an understanding (of Being)
    through a direct vision of its wizardry
And (the time has come) to attend creatively to this
    wizardry (taking place) in a mood of unreality,
In the preliminary (to the actual practice), as has been
    detailed in the previous case, you have to pray to be
    enabled to deal competently with this wizardry.[15]

BIIa   In actual practice, (you have to note that) the variety of
    the without and within
Presents itself as an enchanting apparition due to the
    power of causes and conditions.
Constantly, from moment to moment, day and night,
    attend to and cultivate it
As being untrue in itself, ephemeral, evanescent.

BIIb1   Whatever may arise, be these the emotions of love and
    hatred or the categories of affirmation and negation,
You should experience them as having no truth and
    being nothing, by declaring them an enchanting
    apparition.
All the things of the external world are such an
    enchanting apparition and, similarly,

The ideas within are like an enchanting apparition.
Since all this has come about under certain conditions,
    and since it is untrue and deceptive, and
Since it is merely a presentation, attend to and cultivate
    it by imaginatively using the analogies illustrating
    this spell-weaving.

When you are about to fall asleep—as has been detailed   BIIb2
    in the previous case—relax
In this reach and range of wizardry, that has in it no
    truth as such and defies all propositions.
Then by knowing that any misleading dreams that
    may occur
Are this weaving of spells (by Being), there will be
    freedom from the craving to take them as real and
    freedom from fear and terror.
Exercise this magic as an enchanting apparition
    —developing it, transforming it,
And travelling over the pure realms in an apparition-
    like manner as done in the previous case.

Thereby, the addiction to Saṃsāra is resolved by itself   BIII
    into its (original) freedom,
And having regained freedom in the wizardry (of
    Being), there is no staying (in either form of its
    enchantment),[16] but there occurs the passing into
    Nirvāṇa (whereby)
The bitendential value of Being, though apparition-like,
    is spontaneously realized.
Therefore attend to this (ultimate) value (that can only
    be experienced) as apparition-like wonderment.

❖❖❖

CHAPTER THREE

Illusion[1]

The interaction between a presence and a response to its challenge, resulting in an interference pattern, reappears on a more concrete level as the interaction between an environment and a cognitive agency, by which a general framework, within which further activities are going to take place, is set up. The cognitive agency itself develops and becomes contextually differentiated into distinct bearers of intentionality such as perceptions, sensations, feelings, volitions, dispositions, thoughts and so on—all of which contribute to the formation and organization of 'constructs' or 'sets of constructs'. One of these constructs is the notion of a self which is assigned a distinct place in the environing world made up of other constructs, all of which can act on each other causally. It is through these constructs that we conceive and perceive and are interested in the world in which the 'subject'—which has become associated with feeling, desires, intentions, and cognitions—is one of the 'objects' populating the world that, unlike the subject-'self', has its specific object-'self', without the feelings and whatever else is supposed to go with the subject-self. Eventually, this constructing and structuring becomes so ingrained that we are lulled into the belief that conceiving and perceiving could not operate otherwise and that the structure of the world corresponds precisely to the conceptual construction of it. Not only does this involve a confusion of abstracted constructs with the informative source, but there seems to be no inherent need to continue in this particular manner and direction, and it is perception itself that points to other possibilities of conceiving and perceiving.

It is a matter of common knowledge that, as we put it, our senses sometimes deceive us. This alone should already destroy the common and deep-rooted notion that perception (this term being used to cover all the senses that may be available to living beings) is a passive process by which sense impressions are allowed to come into us, where they are assembled into whole structures. Rather, the percipient himself has to do many things and it is his action, including his movement and postures, that aids in setting up and, subsequently, supplying a certain general structure to what he perceives. In other words, the environment, which implicitly contains all the information about the structure which we are going to call the world, is the ever-present stimulus for the construction of it in our perception of it, whereby a certain similarity between the structure of our perceptions and the structure of our world is established. But since this similarity is not perfect we are continually confronted with what is not contained in earlier perceptions, and this implies that there is more in the 'world' than what we have perceived so far. Such instances of confrontation are, among others, illusions and hallucinations, the difference in them being that in the case of illusions we perceive things the way they are not, while in that of hallucinations we perceive what is not even there.

Despite this disquieting frequency we tend to dismiss illusions and hallucinations as trivial, simply because we have selected one possibility, among many others, of dealing with the 'world', and in so doing we have lost sight of the fact that our selection is merely a hypothesis which, it must be admitted, has been confirmed by countless experiences that fitted into its particular framework and did not raise any problems or doubts. To recognize illusions and hallucinations as significant does not mean that they eventually will or should supersede our 'veridical' perceptions and that we then should categorically state that the universe (ourselves included) is a gigantic hallucination (which may be true in the sense that, as quantum field theory suggests, the universe is a 'vacuum fluctuation' of the void, coming out of it and returning to it without leaving any trace). Rather, illusions and hallucinations point to a 'quality of existing' that has been overlooked in, if not radically excluded from, the habitual 'reality system' of mere quantification. They do not represent the intensely felt value of Being; they only facilitate the recovery of this feeling by exposing the dubiousness and shallowness of the merely quantitative and mechanistic. Illusions and hallucinations re-introduce feeling (which on the quantitative level is confused with judgment of feeling) and pave the way for tuning-in to the life-process and becoming whole again.

*L*isten to my explication of the Victorious One's statement that
(All that is) is like an optical illusion.

In the same way as there arises from a visible object an AIa
optical illusion,
So also by the power of the vagaries of inveterate
tendencies, there comes from the dynamic reach
and range that is Mind-as-such,
The optical illusion of Saṃsāra—there being nothing
and yet there being a presence[2]—a state of utter
mistakenness.
This, in whatever (concrete content) it presents itself, is
like an optical illusion.[3]

Foolish are the unregenerate persons, deceived by their AIb
craving for reality—
Look how they are lost by taking what has no value as
a self,
Once they have been enmeshed in the jungle of the
illusions set up by the five sensory objects.

The world of appearances and our fictions about it, the AIIa
physical world and the living beings in it, happiness
and misery, heights and depths,
Have never existed as such—yet are a presence, like the
shadow cast by a lamp,
A double image when the eyeball is pressed, or the
dark night (of) the thick crowd of the emotions.
All this is present as long as it is not critically
scrutinized, but when it is scrutinized, it eludes our
grasping it concretely;

And if it is still more carefully scrutinized, it passes
　　beyond all limitations (constructed by the
　　noetic-noematic complex).
This very moment understand this (break-through) as
What is meant by primordial meaningfulness,[4] unborn,
　　like the sky.

AIIb　This mistaken presentation (of Saṃsāra) has no
　　　foundation and is like an optical illusion,
　　It has no roots and no connotative significance
　　　whatsoever.
　　When scrutinized it turns out to be nothing—without
　　　there being (anything), yet there being a presence.
　　Understand this unoriginatedness of its actuality as
　　　primordiality.

AIIc　In the same way as in a vast plain
　　　What is small appears to be large,
　　So also by the tiniest belief in what is not a self as a self
　　There comes this vast mistaken presence of Saṃsāra.

AIId　If you understand this presence as a mistaken identity,
　　　(you will find that) it has nothing substantial about
　　　it (which you might repudiate).
　　And when it is clear (to you) that, as with the sky, there
　　　is no doing (away with it),
　　Then just let be without taking as a self what has
　　　no value
　　Apart from being a fiction, like an optical illusion, by
　　　virtue of there being a presence without there being
　　　anything.

AIIe　It is the dynamic reach and range (of Being as
　　　experience); it is the beginningless beginning; it has
　　　been pure since its very beginning.
　　Do not believe it to be anything (particular); do not
　　　introduce a division (into it).

What is the point of nailing it down with the craving for
     demarcations,
When it is but a presence that cannot be concretized?
Therefore dismiss all speculation about it.
Know what is present to be devoid of any truth
     principle.

When you thus have understood that all that is is like   BI
     an optical illusion,
Let Mind-as-such be as it is in itself.
As has been detailed previously, first pray to be able to
     deal competently with this optical illusion.

Then comes the creative attention to all that is as an   BIIa
     optical illusion.
Colors and forms are devoid of any truth principle, and
     are like an illusion;
Sounds are devoid of any sound-principle, and are like
     an illusion;
Fragrances, flavors, tactile pressures are like an illusion
And the (subjective) mind with its ideas is like an
     illusion.
Let your intellectual activity, without (feeling) the urge
     to interfere, relax
In this dynamic reach and range where there is no truth
     principle (to restrict it).

As during daytime, so also when you go to sleep,   BIIb
     concentrate mind (on the light) in the heart region
And then fall asleep where all that is is like an optical
     illusion.
Certainly there will come such experiences as those
     (which have been detailed in the discussion of the
     state) when dreaming has been taken hold of.

Even the presence of experiencing and of   BIII
     understanding[5] is like an optical illusion,

When by the force of the presence the (ultimate)
understanding has come that nowhere is there
any truth principle.
The mistaken identification (of Being) (effected)
through negation and affirmation breaks down,
and there is no longer any subjective
interference.
(Thus) the capabilities for and qualities of wider
visions, higher perceptions, and (other) holistic
experiences have become operative,
And (as) the treasure of Buddhahood, they lead all
sentient beings.
Therefore, creatively attend to what (is meant by the
statement that all that is) is like an optical illusion.

CHAPTER FOUR

Mirage[1]

Among the numerous illusions and hallucinations that occur in and attend our experience, a mirage may be said to have a special place. From a scientific point of view a mirage depends on atmospheric conditions. The vision of a pool of water is created by light passing the layers of hot air above the heated surface of a desert or even a highway. Since air cools rapidly with elevation and therefore increases in density and refractive (bending) power, these cooler layers of air refract the sun's rays at different angles from the less dense or rarified strata of heated air. The effect is that to the observer there appears water where there is none. Nearby objects, such as trees or telephone poles, may even appear to be reflected in the 'water', and this adds to the complexity of the mirage.

The special place held by the mirage lies in the fact that it operates on a larger scale. It is well known that emotions, compelling associations, feelings of anxiety and fear, and strong expectations contribute to the emergence of illusions and hallucinations. The mistaken identification of one thing as another is a limited, though common, misperception in everyday life, but a mirage is felt as the unfolding of a whole panorama. As in the previous case of illusions and halluci-nations, the point here is to make us realize that our 'nor-mal' state is one of inhibitions and one which deprives us of much that is full of 'magic' which is needed in the search for meaning.

Again, listen to my explication of the Victorious One's statement that
All that is is like a mirage.

In the same way as at noon in the hot season
There appears on a plain the water in a mirage,
So also by the power of habituation to a belief in the
    mind as a self
The mistaken presence of the fictions (about the world)
    comes like a mirage.

As to its facticity, there is nothing that could be grasped
    concretely,
And as to its actuality, there is no duality in it; it
    remains an open and calm quality.
Know that that which has not come into (concretized)
    existence is like the sky and has no ontological
    principle,
And that that which has no origin lies beyond the
    constructs of the mind.

In whichever way it may present itself, from that time
    onwards when it presented itself,
It has appeared as coming into existence, but it remains
    unoriginated, like a mirage;
It has appeared as abiding, but it does not abide, similar
    to a mirage;
It has appeared as (having) ceased, but it has not done
    so, like a mirage;
Know that that which is thus present has no essence.

AIIc   Joys and sorrows, happiness and misery, good and evil
Are all like a mirage, an open (possibility) without an
     ontological principle.
All that is—the world of the within and the without,
     together with the fictions about it—is like a mirage.
While there is nothing there is yet a presence[2] and as
     this has been free from its very beginning in its
     actuality—
Understand it as an open (possibility) from the very
     beginning, having neither center nor periphery.

AIId   To take that which has no duality as a duality is like a
     mirage.
Without allowing yourself to become fettered by the
     craving for affirming or negating what has no
     real value,
View your mind as having no duality, as being like a
     mirage.
This is the intentionality of the Buddhas of the three
     aspects of time.

BI   Then, in the procedure for attending creatively to
     this topic,
The preliminary stage, as previously detailed, is to pray
     to be able to deal competently with a mirage.

BII   In actual practice, let the mind settle—without going
     outward or turning inward, without expectation
     or fear—
In the dynamic reach and range in which all that is is
     like a mirage.
Also at night, when you scrutinize this as before, the
     experience will be felt as a mirage.

BIII   When there is no craving for anything, the belief in
     (any form of) a self unravels itself by itself.

Clouds of spiritual sustenance,[3] higher perceptions,
  and holistic experiences arise from deep within.
Since the citadel of the Victorious One is quickly
  reached,
Attend creatively to what in its actuality is like a
  mirage.

CHAPTER FIVE

The Reflection
of the Moon in Water[1]

The occurrence of illusions and hallucinations, regardless of the culturally (societally) sanctioned attitude of acceptance or rejection, challenges the adequacy of the habitual patterns through which we tend to perceive our world and ourselves. This occurrence may well be a call for a reordering of our understanding of all that concerns us in our life, by allowing novel patterns to evolve through which an increased sensitivity and awareness could be facilitated. Any such reordering, however, is only too often resisted by the diffuse tendency to adhere to habitual patterns. Opting for an elusive but dynamic universe in which we would continue learning, rather than dispensing stale trivialities, and in which our life would proceed with the life forces in and around us, is tantamount to rejecting a secure but static universe which in its dullness and monotony can hardly be said to be satisfactory.

It may not always be obvious but monotony is the keynote in any of the many 'explanations' of the phenomenon of life and even of experience, because all explanations involve

a kind of reductionism. If what we perceive is not what we habitually (and uncritically) believe it to be, might this disquieting feature not simply be resolved by resorting to an ideal state of utter annihilation or, in modern terms, maximum entropy? Might not another way of looking do justice to what is actually going on? This other way is the awareness that the entities—which seem to have form, a discrete and fixed spatial configuration, and a continuous sustenance through time—are a process and that apart from process there is no being. Being thus becomes synonymous with the experience of its dynamic process, and if experience is understood as a dynamic process, certain ontological features are implicitly present. Being itself, rather than being as a static entity, becomes a dynamic presentation, and experience becomes its explication in perceptual, conceptual and valuational reciprocity. In order to be able to perform this ongoing act of presentation, Being must be 'nothing' from the ordinary way of thinking that deals with concrete entities as a closed system. Being is never some static nothingness and, therefore, by implication, its experience of itself as process retains an 'open' character that structures the evolving universe by suggesting a plan which is subsequently given concrete content by an active response and creative participation in it.

Such an event-structure or unity of processes, incorporating the influences of all events—including the ingression of mind as intrinsical to them, their antecedents, contemporaries, and descendents—is 'the reflection of the moon in water'. Rather than emphasizing futility, this experience adds fresh meanings to man's life, meanings to be achieved within the intentionality of experience which becomes determined and which determines itself in finite images.

*A*gain I shall explicate the Victorious One's
statement that (all that is) is like the reflection
of the moon in water
In order that this may be experienced.

In the center of the deep and glistening ocean of   A1a
    Mind-as-such
There resides (its) spontaneity (that is) the images that have
    displayed themselves since (their) very beginning;
But it is owing to contamination by the turbid waves of
    subject and object
That it does not shine brightly and is lashed by the wind
    of divisive concepts.
Since the delusion of the world has sprung from the
    belief in (it as) a Self,
Pristine cognitiveness has lost its shining quality, has
    become non-cognitive and has turned into
    emotionality,
And (so) it has submerged in Saṃsāra, that has neither
    beginning nor end.[2]

In the same way as the reflection of the stars in clear   A1b
    water
Glistens steadily (as the paradox of) there being nothing
    and yet there being a presence,
So also the images of the mistaken presence (of the
    world), arising in the water of the mind (in this
    paradox of)
There being nothing and yet there being a presence,
    wear out sentient beings.

Since this (presence) is nothing substantial, it cannot be   A1c
    grasped.
Since this (presence) is nothing qualitative, it cannot be
    characterized.

(Since) it is neither something existent nor non-existent,
   it is beyond the limits of true and false,
This is what is meant by speaking of 'images'.

AIIa   Color-form and so on[3] are like the reflection of the
      moon in water:
   Because of (this paradox of) there being nothing and
      yet there being a presence, and because of (the fact)
      that nothing solid can be found, and
   Because observable qualities do not cease (to present
      themselves), and because there is a presentation in
      this domain of mistaken identification,
   The eye, the controlling power of the eye, and the
      visual cognition (taking place)
   Are like the reflection of the moon in water—nothing,
      vain and hollow—
   Like a delusion with no hard core to it (like) a plantain.[4]
   Understand all observable qualities as devoid of any
      truth principle.

AIIb   Mind—not shrouded by limiting categories (of the
      intellect) and untainted (by its demands)—
   Is a presence and yet nothing, defying (all attempts to
      capture it in) propositions, as is the case of the
      reflection of the moon in water.
   Know it to be profound, calm, not divided (by
      concepts), a pristine cognitiveness, passing
      beyond words,
   Radiant in itself, and steady in its glow.

AIIc   In the same way as when the water appears as the
      moon, the water is not the moon,
   So also when the multiplicity (of the world) makes its
      presence felt, this multiplicity is not something that
      can be established or dismissed.
   Let it be just as it is without introducing a division,

Free from the intellectual activity that is concerned with
    the conventions of the three aspects of time.

Do not prejudge this mind in and as limpid clearness   AIId
    and consummate perspicacity, which in its totality
    knows of no coming or going,
Which has neither a without nor a within, and which
    passes beyond (the reaches of) purposive thinking.
Stop the frantic search for wideness or narrowness,
    exaltedness or lowliness
In what is undisrupted and does not become partial.[5]

This primordial reach and range (of experience) that   AIIe
    cannot be thought of (as anything) and does not stay
    as a single (entity),
Is a whole (in) whatever (experience) it comes, and it is
    like the reflection of the moon in water.
Let your thinking settle where this reach and range is
    just as it is
And where Saṃsāra and Nirvāṇa are alike, neither true
    nor false.

The configurations that present the world of appearance   AI
    and the fictions about it, Saṃsāra and Nirvāṇa, in
    the glow of the reflection of the moon in water,
Have been nothing (as such) from the very beginning,
    are nothing by virtue of there occurring no
    sedimentation, and are nothing in their actuality
    that has been there from the very beginning.[6]
Since you will become mistaken about them due to the
    postulates of existence and non-existence by the
    intellect,
Do not cling to axioms that introduce distinctions and
    partialities.

As long as there is the intellect with its clinging to   AIIg
    an ego,

There is no chance to find freedom from Saṃsāra.
Without subjective interference, settled in itself, fresh
    and genuine, mind at rest
Is wide, settled from its very beginning, free in itself,
    expanding far and wide.
What is the point of introducing an artificiality into it?

AIIh   Objects have nothing in themselves (to make them
    objects) and are like the reflection of the moon
    in water;
When likewise the mind (devoid of any clinging) arises
    without interfering with them,
Then, since where there is neither subject nor object,
    there is no relationship between an object and
    a mind,
This (event) is the reach and range of utter
    completeness, where no efforts (to find out what it
    is) are necessary.

AIIi   Whatever comes as a friend
Is spontaneously felt as unbiased great bliss.
Once you know it thus, without there being any place
    to go to,
You proceed to the primordial ground of limpid
    clearness and consummate perspicacity.

AIIj   To remain in this dynamic reach and range, once you
    have understood it in this manner,
Is the steady application of creative imagination which
    is like the reflection of the moon in water.
A person fortunate (enough to understand this) must
    thoroughly familiarize himself with the fact
That in whatever form (experience) may present itself,
    this form has no truth principle in it; it is
    ephemeral and floating.

The preliminary is, as in the previous instances, to pray   BI
to be able to deal competently with the experience
of the reflection of the moon in water.
The main procedure is to become composed in a state
of thinking
That whatever presents itself is like the reflection of the
moon in water.

At night, as in the previous instances, but here in   BII
particular, the experience of the reflection of the
moon in water
Must remain in this overarching unitary reach and
range, without any subjective interference.

Quickly the throne of the king, Mind-as-such, has been   BIII
occupied.
When you look at whatever presents itself, you remain
free from taking it as some particular presence.
There rises a sheer lucency that is like the reflection of
the moon in water, radiant in its glow.
This is what a most fortunate person should attend to.

CHAPTER SIX

Echo[1]

The assumption that the world process will inexorably move in the direction of a final state of utter annihilation is only one aspect of the reductionism that is so characteristic of rational cognition which because of this limitation is inadequate as an exclusive tool for spiritual growth. Although not always recognized for what it actually is, this reductionism manifests itself in other impoverishing and narrowing aspects of thought. In his attempt to understand the complexity and complicatedness of his world, man has devised artifices which enter into and shape all immediate experiences in such a way that they become inseparable from them. Because of this fusion, which is rather a confusion of the structured features of the artifices with the features of the world as an ongoing process of presentation for abstraction and construction, it is usually forgotten that an artifice has been constructed and, as a consequence, this artifice is taken to have universal validity because it is compatible with the observed invariant features in an individual's experience of his world. The construct or artifice thus corresponds to and represents a static mechanistic universe, which is made up of allegedly eternal and immutable essences. Such a universe is addressed by the objectifying question 'what is it?', and in the attempt to have a detached view of the world the most important question of 'who is asking the question?' is suppressed, because the inclusion of the actor (subject) in the process would upset the oversimplification of it into 'objective truth'.

Despite the high esteem in which essences, representative of a static cosmos, are held in reductionist philosophical thinking, be this realism with its postulation of an 'objective' realm of eternal essences or idealism with its regression to a transcendental 'subject' which nevertheless remains an 'object' in the universe of entities, they are totally hypothetical. The more one looks for them and tries to pinpoint them, the more elusive they become. This search is like the attempt to find the core of an onion by peeling one layer after the other. Of course, no core is found, and even if it were possible to locate an essence as a kind of formal and common denominator, how could we, without already having prejudged the whole matter, derive or establish a distinct property such as man's 'rational animality'? Similarly, to say of material things that their essence is to be material is merely begging the question. As a construct or artifice, an essence is the product of the intentionality of mind as process, not as an entity, which occasions the emergence of meanings with which we deal in life. This intentionality contradicts the very notion of a stable essence of any particular thing. What we call a 'thing' is always a plurality of perspectives and intentions occurring within the process of intending, and thereby leading to 'structure' (essence) which is kept fluid and 'open' by the process.

Any 'what' question of the kind 'what is the nature of that which is?' is coupled with a peculiar world-picture of objectifiable entities differentiated from each other by specifically essential predicates. Necessarily much that is relevant to the living person is left out in such a universe and any such substantializing and essentializing conceals the participation of the inquirer in the process of learning about his universe. Hence a reductionist 'what' question is one-sided and has to be replaced by the more pertinent question of 'how does the process of interaction between the observer as an active participant and the observed as an equally active solicitation proceed in forming a single relationship of meaning?' But where does one look to see the process operate? The answer is to the process itself which is experience. In the de-essentializing and desubstantializing of experience so as to restore it to its dynamic movement, the analogy of an echo is a valuable aid.

*A*gain listen to my clear explication of the
Victorious One's statement
That (all that is) is like an echo.

In the same manner as the voices of persons near rocks   AIa
    and mountains
Are brought back as an echo,
So also all that is has nothing substantial about it.
Understand it thoroughly to be devoid of any truth
    principle.[2]

Even if you search for the sound of the echo in   AIb
The without, the within, and the in-between, you will
    not find it.
So also, if you have intellectually (rationally)
    investigated all that is, be this the without or the
    within—
All that presents itself through the working of mind and
    mental events—
Be this on a coarse (macroscopic) or subtle level,[3] you
    will find nothing (of an essence).
(Everything) is open like the sky, without any
    substantiality, and transparently pure;
If you understand (everything) in this way, you will not
    hanker after and hold to anything.

Even the belief in two realities—which states that   AIc
Things are there for all practical purposes, but
    ultimately they are not found so—is a split set up by
    the intellect;
Yet from that time onwards when something made its
    presence felt, it has (remained in the range that)
    passes the intellect.

This network of propositions set up by the intellect is
one's own mind.
That in which there is no interference by a network of
concepts,
Because nowhere is any waxing or waning in
importance introduced in the objects (created by the
mind), cannot be grasped concretely.
When you know it in this way, you go beyond (the
limitations imposed by) propositions.

AId   Out of the primordial Mind-as-such, which is like the
vast sky or the Wish-fulfilling Gem, and
Out of its immaculate ocean which is the spontaneity of
all capabilities,
There comes the world of fictions, having as the
condition for its presence the loss of pure awareness
with its proliferation of divisive concepts, and
Like an echo—there being nothing and yet a
presence—it roams about here.
The self-manifestation (of Being as the presence) of the
six kinds of sentient beings occurs through the
power of the inveterate tendencies.
One's own mind, sullied (by these tendencies), identifies
itself with (its fictions) through the power of its
tendency of identification.

AIe   Under these circumstances, the presence mistaken for
sentient beings and for mind
Is an actuality that has no foundation as such and has
no root whatsoever.
Ah! how funny is this paradox of there being nothing
and yet there being a presence.
What is the point of hankering after and holding to a
truth principle
In what presents itself as a value but is only like the
sound of an echo,
By taking as a value what has no value whatsoever?

Whatever something may be, let it be in the one
overarching reality that has nothing to which one
can hold on.
Whatever makes its presence felt suddenly, let it
remain free where no truth principle (restricts
freedom).
There is every reason to be happy because there is
neither (something) wide nor narrow, neither high
nor low.

Affirmation and negation, as to what presents itself in   AIIa
such a way that no intention as to what has arisen is
entertained,
Come like an echo.
When what something is has found the freedom where
there is nothing to hold on to,
Then it is (what it is), the one overarching reality, free
of every margin.

Ha, ha, look how funny is this mistaken presence!   AIIb
Since its factuality cannot be grasped concretely, it is
elusive,
Tenuous, paradoxical, evasive, casual;
Improbable, with no intent or truth, it yet is present in
many ways.[4]

For the stupid it seems to be real, because of their   AIIc
desirousness to have it real.
For the yogi who knows its unreality, it is one
overarchingness.
For those who believe the transitory to be eternal, it
seems to be eternal,
For whose who are free from the belief in eternalism, it
is just an open-dimensional imagery.
They are happy because there is nothing to be split up
into (something) wide or narrow.

BI   The way of becoming habituated to and acquainted
     with what is to be understood is as follows:
     The preliminary, as in the previous instances, is to pray
     for being able to deal competently with an echo,
     The actual procedure is to imagine all that is to be like
     an echo,
     That from the time it is heard it cannot be grasped
     concretely,
     And that whatever presents itself is of the same nature.

BII   In particular, praise and blame, and melodiousness and
     dissonance
     Are devoid of any 'sound' reality principle, and cannot
     be grasped concretely.
     Since any affirmation or negation of them by the mind
     is meaningless,
     Understand sounds to be like an echo.

BIII The mind (tainted by) anger and other emotions is
     neither in the object nor in any direction (of the
     compass).
     When it is there, since there is nothing, one does not
     find it by searching for it.
     Anything that has arisen due to conditions and is
     nothing (in itself) is like the sound of an echo.
     Even the words (spoken by) an opponent arise due to
     conditions and are like an echo,
     If you investigate them, they are a mere
     reflection—there being nothing and yet a presence;
     If you investigate them still more, they are like the sky
     with no substantiality in them.
     Since neither good nor evil, neither falling nor rising, is
     observed,
     Do not hold sound to have any value in itself; it is
     devoid of any truth principle.
     Understand everything observable to be like an echo.

In this way the inveterate tendencies, that have since
 beginningless time led to Saṃsāra, (cease to be
 active), and
Specifically the fire of anger and hatred is extinguished,
And one acquires the letting-be (Gelassenheit)[5] of the
 noble and does not fall into evil existences.
Gradually one comes close to the riches of the
 Victorious One.

At night, as has been detailed previously, think of the
 echo (character) in particular;
Acquire this letting-be (in which) sound has no truth
 principle.
Therefore, attend to what is meant to be like an echo.

CHAPTER SEVEN

Cloud Land[1]

*E*ven if it be admitted, though reluctantly, that there can be no stable essences because what a thing is depends on the varied and changing perspectives of the observer, the tendency to look for something invariant and immutable remains strong. Thus the notion of invariance and immutability, characteristic for a static cosmos, survives, in a subtler form, in the assumption of 'facts' which as facts about something are reducible to properties and relations. Again, reductionism, which dominates rational thought, is operative and in no way changes the restrictive picture of the world as a 'totality of entities', be these on a cruder level 'substances' and 'essences', and on a subtler one 'facts'.

'Cloud-lands' or more literally, 'cities of ethereal beings', are neither isolated objects having an eternal essence nor absolute facts, but rather occurrences that can be understood and appreciated as complex wholes in which the observer as a participant is deeply involved by marking out possible meanings and excluding others. This does not mean that he is the sole originator of the emergent meanings but that the experienced world is one in which anticipations and recollections are already simultaneously at work. The vision of a cloud-land is anticipatory in the sense that our expectations may be fulfilled, and it is recollective in the sense that 'cities' offered varied entertainment. The emphasis, however, is on the experience itself which is value-orientated, rather than object-orientated. Although sight is most susceptible to objectification and essentialization, in its mediating a perceptual experience, it is indissolubly linked with the experiencer's projected purposes and preoccupations, not so much as ego-centered fixations but as overall directions of spiritual growth. It is experience that speaks to us more profoundly than any quantification which by its overestimation of measurement (the reduction to scale) greatly diminishes human existence. The experience of the perception of what is termed a cloud-land, vividly illustrates the existential evidence value[2] indicative of the intensity of the experience of that which is mediated—by sight in this case. A cloud-land can be easily 'seen' as having no reality value, which is indicative of the degree to which a sense transmits material resistance, and yet as having a very high existential evidence value, not merely directed at the environment but including the experience of our own nature and existence.

*A*gain, listen to my explication of the Victorious One's statement that
(All that is) is like a cloud-land, so that (this topic) also may be experienced.

AIa   In the sky(-like) space of primordial sheer lucency
An ornate city, (Being's) spontaneous capabilities, appears and
Is present in what has neither beginning nor end nor a center nor a periphery.

AIb   Out of the dynamic reach and range of this (openness and lucency) there arise in the sky of the mind, which is the loss of pure awareness,
The cloud-lands of the six kinds of beings that have their origin in the subject-object division.
They are present without having a founding basis of their own, and their manifold forms
Have been born from subjectivity gone astray in and through inveterate tendencies.

AIIa   When this is understood, it is the primordial reach and range of Mind-as-such;
When it is not understood, it is the present mind (having become mistaken about itself and) gone astray.
Since it cannot be grasped in any way that would do justice to it,
What other analogy than a cloud-land could be found for it?

AIIb   However, all this has no essence and so
Is like the cloud-land over a desert at evening time.

The duality of a founding (stratum) and a founded
(structure) is the mind (having become mistaken
about itself and) gone astray.
If it is understood that this is its inveterate tendency,
the mind is found to have no factual reality.
If it is left as it is (by itself), to that extent it remains
naturally free.
Therefore it should not be difficult to relinquish one's
apprehensions about it.
Know this fictitious world and the living beings in it to
have been nothing as such and pure from the very
beginning.

All that appears as objects is devoid of a truth principle,   AIIc
a cloud-land;
All intellectual operations are devoid of any
sedimentation—a cloud-land.
Since what appears as the duality of object and mind is
like a cloud-land,
Let any hankering after and holding to it, however
small, be in its proper place.

That which presents itself without actually existing—   AIId
Do not stir it up by the intellect and do not read
anything into it.
Since even the beginningless going-astray has
originated from the craving to hold (to it),
Know now the actuality (which confronts you) to have
no subjectively predetermined intention in it.

Since of those things that are noble and unfailing,   AIIe
Nirvāṇa in its peacefulness, has nothing substantial
about it,
You should know that all that is (termed) substance and
non-substance
Is devoid of any truth principle and is like a cloud-land
or the expanse of the sky—

Thoroughly calm from its very beginning and without (the urge to) come into existence.

AIIf Desire is not observed there, neither is there aversion;
Dullness, arrogance, envy are (likewise) not observed.
When you know that what is possessed of proliferating ideas is like a cloud-land,
There cannot but be the understanding that the emotions as having no factual existence and
Mind-as-such as limpid clearness and consummate perspicacity, in their non-duality, are like the sky with no impurity.[3]

AIIg Saṃsāra has been for ever Nirvāṇa—
The calming down of the mistaken notion about it is like the dispersal of the clouds in the sky.
Once you know this coming to rest in the primordial birthplace,
Preserve the pristine cognitiveness—utterly calm, open and radiant, in this its reach and range.

AIIh Although the objects as intended (by the subjective mind) are not found in the reach and range that has no origination,
Without suppressing the magic of this origination
You should cut the root of the going astray into proliferating concepts.
Although there is neither something to be done nor not to be done, neither acceptance nor rejection,
As long as there is the mind believing in substance and a self,
You must rely on the profound message as a means to counteract the emotions.
When you thus understand freedom in or as the reach and range of Mind-as-such, in which neither a within nor a without exist,
You have become a wise person.

Now, when you actually are about to imagine creatively   BI
    what has been explicated,
The preliminary must be the same as in the previous
    instances, and the actual procedure
Is to encounter all that is as a cloud-land.

Forms are nothing and yet a presence—a cloud-land;   BII
Sounds, fragrances, flavors, tactile pressures, and ideas
    are a cloud-land.
Let mind and the categories of assertion and
    negation come;
Imagine them clearly as the reach and range of a
    cloud-land.
Accustom yourself, as before, at all times, day
    and night,
To the fact that all that is present is a cloud-land.

Once you have seen things as a cloud-land and as   BIII
    contrived,
By letting them be in the reach and range that has no
    truth principle, all propositions subside;
The self-existent sheer lucency, open and radiant, rises
    out of its depth.
Even in dreams (their images) are seen as cloud-lands;
The attention to developing and transforming (these
    experiences) is as before—
Since one is free from the hankering after a truth
    principle, the subject-object fetter is broken.
Freedom, in which the tendencies that link up with all
    and everything have fully ceased to be operative, is
    obtained.
Therefore creatively imagine this cloud-land (character
    of all that is).

CHAPTER EIGHT

Phantoms[1]

ationality, which serves an important function within the total life of the mind, is not only self-maximizing but also tends to usurp dominance over all other functions and even to suppress those that have a high existential evidence value, such as inspirations, insights, intuitions, imaginations and visions. It does so by luring us deeper and deeper into the barren wastes of its imposing constructs—increasingly regular and rigid patterns—and making us overlook the fact that the genesis of such constructs, which can only serve as a model of reality but are never reality itself, owes a great deal to what is not rationality. Confronted with its own failure to find any abiding essence which would differentiate one thing from another in splendid isolation, it at once rushes into the fallacious conclusion that there must obtain absolute identity. Identity, like difference, the one being the co-implicate of the other, is a static concept applicable only to a static or mechanical cosmos that leaves little room for experience as a dynamic process. Any process is a many-splendored unfolding of its in-built potentials that in their unfolding assume different qualities, values, and meanings which are not, however, disruptive of the complexity of the process but are life-enhancing as they proceed and develop in a phantom-like manner. They only become a dead burden when reduced to isolated constructs which attempt to eliminate the variables and break up the very complexity of the living process.

A phantom, in particular, is a phenomenon that remains nothing in the sense that as an 'openness' it allows a dynamic process to extend its range of action, and yet it also is a presence which is 'closed' in the sense that its solicitations for a reaction to it are such that the reactions occur in strictly determined ways. As a presence it has the further characteristics of either a 'pure' presence or an 'impure' one in which the ongoing process is changed and processed by itself, in such a way that it fights the tendency towards becoming a dead construct by preserving the very knowledge by which the creative process as process is maintained.

The significance of the analogy of a phantom lies in the fact that a phantom undermines the rigidity of old patterns of perceiving and of thinking and points to a structuring process of a higher-order level. The phantom, therefore, may be thought of as process facing two worlds. One is the ordinary external world as the 'what' of the presentation; the other is the internal world which reflects the 'how' of the on-going process. This can alter from moment to moment, as either remaining 'pure' or becoming 'impure', in which case a further distortion is added to the 'what' by the emergence, introduction, and participation of subjectivity or selfhood. Like the other analogies, a phantom is not an end in itself or an answer to the problem of Being, but a freeing device to facilitate access to the very source of being.

*A*gain listen to my explication of the Victorious
One's statement
That all that is is a phantom.

AIa The various mistaken presentations of Saṃsāra that
         have issued
   From the loss of pure awareness, the belief in a Self—
   (Proceeding) from the reach and range that from its
         beginningless beginning has been a sheer lucency—
         are like phantoms.
   This paradox of there being nothing and yet there being
         a presence is indulged in by individual experiences
         of happiness and suffering.

AIb This is the inveterate tendency, manifesting itself as
         sentient beings and world:
   When it is pure, there are present through (this)
         self-manifestation in (the individual's make-up) the
         three founding strata as well as
   The pristine cognitions in sheer lucency.
   It has been stated in the *sGyu-'phrul-dra-ba*
   That mind and pristine cognitiveness are the two
         aspects of a self-manifesting process.[2]

AIc The primordial continuum is the birthplace of
         everything;
   When through pure awareness its impurity has been
         made pure, there is pristine cognitiveness;
   Through loss of pure awareness, there occurs the going
         astray into the belief in a Self.
   With the emergence of mind, the six kinds of beings
   In their happiness and suffering appear like phantoms.

Just as a phantom arises from what has no foundation,   Ald
So also know the mistaken presentations to have no
    foundation and to be pure.
Just as a phantom dominates the mind,
So also know the various beings and their minds to be a
    habituation.
Just as a phantom will present itself as one desires it to
    appear,
So also know that all that is comes from causes and
    conditions.
Just as a phantom is a mistaken identification (of) the
    paradox of there being nothing and yet there being a
    presence,
So also know that all that presents itself to a mind is the
    intellect going astray—
Presenting itself by itself, having arisen by itself, having
    the power to make our own mind identify itself
    with it.
As one accustoms oneself to these presentations, so they
    have made their presence felt.

If without giving in to anything you just let be,   Ale
Without going astray anywhere, you remain with the
    ground.
Just as it did previously, Mind-as-such gathers in its
    continuum.

The three poisons or the five poisons,[3] as the case may   Allai
    be, have arisen from proliferating concepts.
Since they are not found (cannot be pin-pointed) when
    investigated,
The emotions are like a phantom, and since they have
    nothing substantial about them,
Let them just be in the reach and range that is unborn
    and open.

AIIaii   However many living beings there may be
in the world of appearances and the fictions
about it, the world as container and the
essences in it—
Each one's physical existence, scope of enjoyment, going
and sitting, happiness and misery
Is like a phantom, not being anything and yet being a
presence, having nothing real about it.
It is not born, it does not cease to exist, it does not
come, it does not go,
It does not step out of itself, it does not change into
something other than itself—rather, it is a
multifarious presence.
Therefore understand it as just a phantom.

AIIaiii   Whatever mistaken notions, with all their painfulness,
abide within the mind
Share in what is like a phantom;
Without there being anything real, their presence
never ceases.
Understand what is devoid of any truth principle to
have no duality.

AIIaiv   The five elemental forces,[4] the world as a container and
the three world spheres as the fictions about the
world, and the beings therein,
With all the affirmation and negation, are set up
phantom-like by the mind.
Even this mind does not exist as such but is merely a
presence, and in its phantom state of exerting its
enchantment
It should be understood as pure from its very
beginning.

AIIbia   For the ignorant unregenerate person, it is present as
concepts and essences;

All the concrete appearances, postulated by the mind as
    substance and quality
Are but the outcome of inveterate tendencies, yet are
    not found really so;
Therefore, without setting up a subject-object division
    with the judgment of 'this' or 'that'
Know everything to be free from limitations and
    beyond words.

Even if one were to speak about and point out all that is   AIIbib
    with statements of 'this' or 'that'
It would but be a hollow name, a hare's horn.
In the ultimate that has nothing concrete about it, it is
    not found and is a mere postulate,
Nothing from all beginning; know it to have no roots
    whatsoever.

Since it is a mere postulate, as the intellect, it does not   AIIbic
    really exist.
The fact that it appears as something really existing is
    due to inveterate tendencies; it is the paradox of
    there being nothing and yet there being a presence.
Since there is no object, there is no subject, and hence
    there is no noetic-noematic complex.
There are no words to express it, no thoughts to
    conceive it, no propositions to define it; it passes all
    limitations.
Since there is none who could point it out as 'this' or
    'that',
Know it to be like a phantom, never having had an
    ontological principle (to make it what it is).

In the same way as a phantom has no tangible reality   AIIbid
    from the time of its appearance,
So also all that is has been devoid of a truth principle.

In the same way as a phantom is beyond the limits set
    up by existence and non-existence,
So also all that is, in itself, is beyond the scope of
    pinpointing it.

AIIbie   In whichever way one may label it—
    Be it as presence, as nothing, as truth, as falsehood—it
    has nothing real about it.
    Without holding it to be 'this' or 'that', look at it as
    absolutely defying any limitations.

AIIbif   When there is no compulsion to hold it to be
    something, whatever something is, it is the whole;
    What is the point of affirming or negating what has only
    nominal validity?

AIIbiia If one holds it to be 'this', it is no longer the experience;
    What can the network of concepts by intellectual
    postulation show?
    The postulates by the mind are the mind's own
    postulates;
    Even if by them the primary, the openness (of Being),
    could be shown,
    Where would be the experience itself, apart from the
    belief in some finality?

AIIbiib Moreover, what is meant by knowing through
    pointing out?
    What there is to be pointed out is what passes beyond
    the pointing out and the pointed-out.
    Therefore, by holding to the compulsive dispute
    over what has no (existential) value,
    Mind-as-such is not understood; there is merely
    intellectual rumination.

The Guru's blessing which enters a person's heart   AIIbiic
Is like the rising of the sun in a cloudless sky.
As soon as through the powerful interrelationship
    it rises,
The real existential value (of Being) is seen.

That which is the overarching unity of all has no fences   AIIci
    set up by speculation that it is or is not 'this'.
Like the sky, free from limits, an open reach, a vast
    expanse—
And in its vastness being there and being nothing—
Know all that is to be just a phantom.

If this mind in which Saṃsāra is a mistaken notion   AIIcii
Is understood, it is Nirvāṇa having been itself from its
    very beginning.
The pristine cognitiveness of pure awareness that has
    no subjective interference may float (in the direction
    of) objects,
But it does not identify itself with the belief that holds
    that which presents itself to it, with no substantiality
    in it, to be this or that.
It remains happily in the dynamic reach and range from
    which the presence (before the mind) and mind
    (taking in the presence) flow forth like phantoms.

If it is understood in this manner, there is nothing else   AIIciii
    to be shown
But this pristine cognition that sees reality. This itself
Has risen by itself and is free in its own right.

It will unfold itself nowhere else but in him   AIIciv
Into whose heart the Guru's grace with thousands of
    devices has entered.
What for those who have eyes becomes a shining lamp
    that lets things appear,
If shown to blind persons—will it illumine anything?

Allcv   Those other people who are even more stupid
        than those
Who do not know words, do not comprehend the
        meaning,
And do not see the bright sun,
Are filled with pride and are like parrots
        repeating words:
They do not catch the real meaning in the network of
        their concepts.
And not knowing it, they are blind men in the
        presence of colors.
There being no occasion for them to understand, they
        take their intellectual deliberation for the real.
Alas! these impetuous persons, so ill-fated,
Will never find the real meaning.
Here, Mind-as-such, the real pristine cognitiveness,
When revealed by the Guru, is seen as the pristine
        cognitions operating in one's own experience;
It comes when one's own mind is put into an unartificial
        state.
It is conspicuous if there is neither expectation or fear,
        neither belief in something nor compulsion (to
        believe in it);
It is still more conspicuous if there is openness-lucency
        with neither a center nor a periphery (to limit it);
But most important is that those who have been graced
        through the succession (of Gurus)
Are taken hold of by the real Guru.

BIa   In unswerving attendance to and creative development
        of the experience (of Being)
The preliminary is, as in previous instances, to tune-in
        to the Guru,
And to pray that one may be capable of dealing with
        the phantom-(like character). The main procedure is
        (to realize that)
The presences before the mind are also like a phantom.

Having decided that everything (retains its character of
    being) unborn and presents itself like a phantom,
Let your mind be where there is no frantic searching for
    it by attention.

At that time, by staying in the reach and range   BIb
That is open and radiant, defying any propositions
    about it, you are free from the distorting
    subject-object division;
There arises a sheer lucency that is like a translucent
    and radiant phantom.
There is no cessation of objects to be presented, but
    there is no artificiality as to taking them as this
    or that.
There is pleasure naturally, shimmering, glimmering,
    undisturbed.
The mind which has become like the sky, radiant, and
    undivided,
Sees its very facticity that is divested of all propositions
    (that attempt to reduce it) to an essence,
While at that time all that is is like a phantom.
The mind's content itself is free in being like a
    phantom.
Attachment, aversion, expectations, fears, and the belief
    in a Self are like phantoms.
There is freedom as ground, path, and goal.

In whatever form one may imaginatively bring it to life,   BIc
    one is not fettered by it.
By imagining it as existing, one is free from the
    eternalistic extreme;
By imagining it as non-existing, one is free from the
    dirt of negativism;
By imagining it as dual, one stays in non-duality;
By imagining it as Self, one is not fettered into the
    belief in a Self;

By imagining it as the other, one is without both
expectations and fears;
By imagining it as 'Developing', it is spontaneously
'Fulfilled';
By imagining it as the Fulfillment Stage, the Developing
Stage is already there phantom-like.[5]

BId   In the simultaneity of rising and being free, one is free
from all emotions;
Having gone beyond subjective ideas, one engages in
this very reach and range of calm and peace,
In the vortex of meaningfulness, when the three
aspects of time do not exist as time—
As in a phantom, not introducing any break in time.

BIe   With the mind not blocked, there is no self-consciousness
(as in) an intoxicated person;
In his spontaneous (reaction) there is no artificiality by
expectations or fear.
Whatever (some thing) is, it is the whole in this
unblocked overarching unity.
(Ultimate) intentionality, encompassing like the sky, is
spontaneously there.

BIIa   When you stay in this reach and range from which day
and night are made to proceed, then
In the control center[6] of pure pleasure, pleasure is a
single cresting.
In the control center of intercommunication, enjoyable
communication with everything is complete.
In the control center of meaning, meaningfulness flows
uninterruptedly.
In the control center of morphogenesis, phantom-like
creations proceed (immeasurably) in inexhaustible
arrays.

In the control center of homeostasis, day and night,
  pleasure protects.
As long as purification has not been achieved, the
  specificity of mentation and motility is attended to;
  (once it has been effected)
The ground on which purification takes place, as well as
  that which has to be purified and the forces of
  purification (taking place through) motility moving
  along the pathways of its flow-patterns (turns into)
The unique flavor of pristine cognitiveness as the
  purified goal having become manifest.

When dreams are induced and transformed the Buddha   BIIb
  realms are seen;
Afterwards deceptive dreams are stopped.
Day and night one stays in sheer lucency.
When you then abide in the reach and range of holistic
  experiences of pleasure, radiance and
  non-dividedness,
Higher visions, higher perceptions, and higher activities
  set in.
Experience and understanding become unbounded and
  the bitendential value (of Being) is realized.
Therefore, fortunate people should always bring to life
  the real value (of life)
In the phantom(-like) presence of all that is.

Epilogue

AI   In order that what the Victorious One has thus
           pointed out
           May be understood as and by eight analogies such
           as Wizardry,
I, Dri-med 'od-zer, have collected the essence of the
           Sūtras, Tantras, and Upadeśas,
And brought it to light.

AII   Through this, my wholesome enterprise, may all
           sentient beings, without exception,
After having seen that all that is is uncreated and like a
           phantom,
Realize ever higher and far-reaching meaningfulness,
And be enriched by tuning in to the three founding
           strata of meaning of the Victorious One.

AIII   Having dismissed the intellectual concern with its
           compulsiveness to hold as true
All that is but like a dream, an enchantment, a mirage,

A reflection, an echo, a phantom—   BI
May they reach the place of pristine cognitiveness with
   its primordial capabilities.

Having gone to delightful groves far away from
The dense jungle of fictions due to
The preoccupation of fools with this-worldly concerns
   and the emotions,
May they become the crown-jewel for countless gods.

May this, my mind, loathing distractions,   BII
Rejoice and remain withdrawn in quiet forest groves
And solely contemplate this profoundness
And acquire the spiritual eyes of the noble.

May this body, endowed with the essential wealth of   BIII
   being a unique occasion and the right juncture,
Be made to walk the way towards freedom found in the
   treasures of [the Buddha's message (about) the real
   value (of life)],
In these forests, beautiful with many flowers, leaves,
   and fruits,
Clear water and the splendors of spiritual
   achievements.

At present, so that I may find my goal,   BIV
I engage in wholesome acts in this realm of men;
Once I am on the path towards inner calm, through
   many capabilities available,
May I set free unlimited beings from this world of
   fiction.

This method is the essence of the profound message,   CI
And since it is the path in which certainty is embedded,
He who wants liberation must exert himself with all
   his heart

And make a living experience of it, without relaxing
either day or night.

CII   May all those who are fortunate in having trust (in the
meaningfulness of Being), in future generations
Rely on these words for all times;
When they have made themselves and others cross the
ocean of fictitious being,
There will be for them spontaneously present the
bitendential value of Being.

CIII   The yogi who has his eyes (opened) by the
profoundness
Of all the meanings found in the Sūtras, Tantras, and
Upadeśas,
Dri-med 'od-zer,
Has composed this work at Gangs-ri thod-dkar, a
necklace of the mountains.

CIV   This sun of meaningful method, having a thousand
stainless rays,
With its light of pristine cognitiveness dispels the
darkness of unknowing
And through it dries up the ocean of Saṃsāra.
This island of freedom, then coming into sight, may
extend into the ten directions.

Notes

NOTES TO INTRODUCTION

1) On this term see the references in *Kindly Bent to East Us*, part I. In his interpretation of this term Klong-chen rab-'byams-pa follows the explanation given in the *Rig-pa rang-shar chen-po'i rgyud* and the *Rin-po-che 'Byung-bar byed-pa sGra-thal-'gyur chen-po'i rgyud*. The former (in *rNying-ma rgyud-'bum,* vol. 10, p. 46) is quoted in both his *Theg-pa'i mchog rin-po-che'i mdzod,* vol. 1, p. 630, and his *Tshig-don rin-po-che'i mdzod,* p. 464.

> Actuality, (the existential immediacy) that has been
> from the very beginning (*ye*), (is) spontaneously given;
> The understanding (of it) has become manifest:
> This is the etymology of 'pristine cognition' (*ye-shes*).

In both quotations by Klong-chen rab-'byams-pa the second line begins with *de-nas* 'then', but the *rNying-ma rgyud-'bum* has *shes-pa* 'by (its) cognition'. Although this latter version seems to be more to the point of the etymology, it remains doubtful whether it is the original reading. The *rNying-ma rgyud-'bum,* reproduced from a hand-written copy, abounds in spelling mistakes, omissions and other defects that mark calligraphic works. In his *Theg-pa'i mchog rin-po-che'i mdzod,* vol. 1, p. 630, Klong-chen rab-'byams-pa paraphrases this verse by saying:

> To know by understanding the meaning of Being that
> has been present from the very beginning.

The 'meaning of Being' is a rendering of *don* 'that which matters' and that which matters can be interpreted on different
levels. *don* is not an analytical term, but points to valuational
relationships. The phrase 'the meaning of Being that has been
present from the very beginning' is from the *sGra-thal-'gyur
chen-po'i rgyud* (*rNying-ma rgyud-'bum*, vol. 10, p. 474):

> The etymology of *ye-shes* is that one now knows (*shes-pa*)
> The meaning of Being that has been present from the very
> beginning (*ye*).

In his *Zab-mo yang-tig*, part 2, p. 217, Klong-chen rab-'byams-pa
quotes the *Thig-le kun-gsal chen-po'i rgyud* (in *rNying-ma rgyud-'bum*,
vol. 5, p. 132) which declares:

> *ye-shes* has not come about incidentally, rather the cognitive
> property of Being that has been present from the very be-
> ginning has taken the lead.

2) There are listed seven such static misinterpretations in
rNying-ma works. See for instance *Theg-pa'i mchog rin-po-che'i
mdzod*, vol. 1, pp. 378d, *mKha'-'gro yang-thig*, part 2, pp. 92 f;
'Jigs-med gling-pa's *rNam-mkhyen shing-rta*, pp. 544 ff, Yon-tan
rgya-mtsho's *Zab-don snang-byed nyi-ma'i 'od-zer*, pp. 371 ff. The
'ground' that is dealt with as an intellectual abstraction is
termed *shes-bya'i gzhi* as contrasted with the 'ground as it is
present in experience' (*gnas-lugs-kyi gzhi*). See *mKha'-'gro snying-
thig*, part E, pp. 341 f, *Bla-ma dgongs-'dus*, vol. 10, pp. 634 f,
647. The *Vima snying-thig*, part Pa, p. 4, distinguishes between
those who follow 'philosophical axioms' (*grub-mtha'*), and
those who pursue the 'way' (*lam*). The diction brings out the
distinction very neatly: 'those who are chasing after philosophical axioms and those who are holding to the way'. The
'way' is always a term for experience.

3) According to *Theg-pa'i mchog rin-po-che'i mdzod*, vol. 1, p. 287,
inseparability (*dbyer-med*) does not involve two discrete entities
that somehow are so closely intertwined as to make a separa-
tion impossible. Basically, it has to do with the problem of
identity as a continuum. The problem is discussed at length in

Bla-ma dgongs-'dus, vol. 5, pp. 66, 806, where six illustrations are given. Nevertheless, the analytical presentation seems to be inevitable as may be seen from the discussion of the 'ground' in *mKha'-'gro snying-thig*, part E, p. 342, part Wam, pp. 35 f; and the various rNying-ma Tantras such as the *Rig-pa rang-shar chen-po'i rgyud* (in *rNying-ma rgyud-'bum*, vol. 10, pp. 167 f), *Mu-tig 'phreng-ba* (ibid., vol. 9, pp. 367 f); *Kun-tu bzang-po klong-drug-pa'i rgyud* (ibid., vol. 13, pp. 628 f), which deal with this problem.

4) This is based on *Vima snying-thig*, part Pa, pp. 3 f. In the following diagrams ‖ signifies 'nowhere else but wholly in'; ⟶ 'soliciting a response'; and ← − − − 'being responded to'.

5) According to *Vima snying-thig*, vol. 1, p. 76, the term *thog-ma* refers to the state before there had evolved the state of Buddhahood through understanding and before there has emerged the state of an ordinary being through lack of understanding, as there had not occurred a slipping from what matters into biasedness.

6) The use of the analogies varies. As a rule, 'facticity' is likened to the clear sky, but 'actuality' may be compared to the brightness of the sun, the moon and the stars, and 'responsiveness' to a polished mirror. See *Bla-ma yang-tig*, part Wam, p. 235. The image of the ocean is used as a simile for the depth of a holistic experience in *Bla-ma dgongs-'dus*, vol. 10, p. 82. A rich array of imagery is employed by Klong-chen rab-'byams-pa and is found in his *mKha'-'gro yang-thig*, vol. 2, pp. 70 ff, vol. 3, pp. 124 f, *Tshig-don rin-po-che'i mdzod*, pp. 28, 102. The one employed above seems to have its literary source in the *Thig-le kun-gsal chen-po'i rgyud*, p. 126.

7) This work is the *Thig-le kun-gsal chen-po'i rgyud* (in *rNying-ma rgyud-'bum*, vol. 5, pp. 124 ff). But in *mKha'-'gro yang-thig* part 2, p. 83, Klong-chen rab-'byams-pa declares that the quotation is taken from the *bsTan-pa rin-po-che gser-gyi yi-ge-can*, a work as yet unidentified.

8) From *mKha'-'gro yang-thig*, part 3, pp. 95 f, it is evident that the primordial Lord 'Immutable Light' is the existential experience

of Being, otherwise referred to by such terms as 'facticity', 'actuality', and 'responsiveness'. See also *Bla-ma yang-tig*, part E, p. 295.

9) In modern terminology, the eternity of empty duration after the end of the world.

10) In modern terminology, the eternity of materially filled duration before the beginning of the world.

11) *Zab-mo yang-tig*, vol. 2, pp. 102 f; *mKha'-'gro snying-thig*, part E, p. 342.

12) See in particular Martin Heidegger, *On Time and Being*.

13) On the various models of the universe in contemporary cosmological theories see Hannes Alfvén, *Worlds-Antiworlds*, pp. 84ff.

14) The 'spontaneous givenness of Being' is said to be 'indeterminate' (*ma-nges-pa*); *mKha'-'gro yang-thig*, part 2, p. 139. That there is no necessity involved is evident from such statements as "although there is no necessity (*rgyu*) for the three kinds of pristine cognitiveness (constituting the ground or Being) to become mistaken about themselves and to go astray, this going astray occurs under the co-determinant (*rkyen*) of not recognizing what is involved for what it is. Just as the sun has no reason or necessity to become darkness, it is by the fog in the atmosphere that it is dimmed." *mKha'-'gro snying-thig*, part E, pp. 350, 486.

15) *mKha'-'gro snying-thig*, part E, p. 348; see also pp. 416, 486; *mKha'-'gro yang-thig*, part 3, p. 172. *Theg-pa'i mchog rin-po-che'i mdzod*, vol. 1, p. 426.

16) The word 'self' is added to make it absolutely clear that no external agency is involved.

17) *gzhon-nu bum-pa'i sku*. This term refers to an existential experience, as is indicated by the term *sku* which, from a different perspective within experience itself, is 'felt' to be a 'founding stratum' on which pristine cognitions are 'founded'. The image of the *bum-pa*—a term that literally translated means 'pot', but

here rendered by 'reservoir'—reflects the Indian idea that only that is 'real' in an ultimate sense which is capable of displaying its content of 'space' (which, however, is never 'empty' in our sense of the word).

Insofar as experience is also a continuum or 'field', the text speaks of a *gzhon-nu bum pa'i sku'i zhing-khams*. On these terms see *Zab-mo yang-tig*, vol. 2, p. 218 which quotes from the *Thig-le kun-gsal chen-po'i rgyud*, p. 133; *mKha'-'gro yang-thig*, part 2, p. 116; part 3, pp. 80, 136, 196; 'Jigs-med gling-pa's *rNam-mkhyen shing-rta*, pp. 553, 559, 804; and Yon-tan rgya-mtsho's explanation of this term in his *Nyi-zla'i sgron-ma*, p. 518.

18) Further details are found in *mKha'-'gro yang-thig*, part 2, pp. 89 f, part 3, pp. 126, 187; in 'Jigs-med gling-pa's *rNam-mkhyen shing-rta* pp. 558 f, and in Yon-tan rgya-mtsho's *Nyi-zla'i sgron-ma*, p. 385.

19) With slight variations this passage occurs in *Theg-pa'i mchog rin-po-che'i mdzod*, vol. 1, pp. 414, 418 f; *mKha'-'gro yang-thig* part 2, p. 102; *Bla-ma yang-tig*, part E, p. 386; part Wam, p. 81; in 'Jigs-med gling-pa's *rNam-mkhyen shing-rta*, p. 560 and in Yon-tan rgya-mtsho's *Nyi-zla'i sgron-ma*, p. 386.

The important point to note is that the two gateways appear simultaneously (*Tshig-don rin-po-che'i mdzod*, p. 29) and thus there is a kind of symmetry between Saṃsāra (a downward directed movement) and Nirvāṇa (an upward directed movement) held together by the spontaneous givenness of Being, but the relationship between the two is asymmetrical in the sense that what appears to be like Nirvāṇa is the ordering principle, while that which appears to be like Saṃsāra is that which is going to be ordered (*Bla-ma yang-tig*, part E, p. 390). In this relationship, which involves interaction, we can easily recognize the recently discovered principle of 'order through fluctuation'. For references see Erich Jantsch, *Design for Evolution*, p. 37.

20) *Theg-pa'i mchog rin-po-che'i mdzod*, vol. 1, p. 404.

21) *mKha'-'gro yang-thig*, part 3, pp. 74 f; part 2, pp. 99 f.

22) On these terms, see Milič Čapek, *The Philosophical Impact of Contemporary Physics*, p. 293 f.

23) Ibid., part 3, p. 74.

24) Ibid., part 3, p. 75.

25) Ibid., part 3, p. 75.

26) *Theg-pa'i mchog rin-po-che'i mdzod*, vol. 1, p. 413.

27) Ibid., p. 418.

28) Ibid., p. 421.

29) Ibid., p. 422.

30) These light values come in various 'frequencies' which account for the various colors which are the prototypes for the 'elemental forces' (*'byung-ba*), eventually becoming what we term 'matter'. See *Theg-pa'i mchog rin-po-che'i mdzod*, vol. 2, p. 3; *Zab-mo yang-thig*, part 2, pp. 254f; *mKha'-'gro snying-thig*, part Wam, pp. 70 f, 111.

31) *Zab-mo yang-thig*, part 2, p. 221.

32) *rNying-ma rgyud-'bum*, vol. 10, p. 96.

33) These three animals, respectively, also represent the emotions of infatuation, irritation and attachment, that underlie the cycle of existence and, in Tibetan paintings of the 'Wheel of Life', are depicted in the innermost circle.

34) *Theg-pa'i mchog rin-po-che'i mdzod*, vol. 1, p. 443.

35) *Theg-pa'i mchog rin-po-che'i mdzod*, vol. 1, pp. 432 f.

36) *Vima snying-thig*, part 2, pp. 340 f.

37) That 'loss of pure awareness' (*ma-rig-pa*) is threefold, is a recurrent theme in rDzogs-chen thought. Here only a few references: *Theg-pa'i mchog rin-po-che'i mdzod*, vol. 1, p. 435; vol. 2, p. 325; *mKha'-'gro yang-thig*, part 2, pp. 120 f, part 3, pp. 187 ff; *Bla-ma dgongs-'dus*, vol. 10, pp. 663, 687, 689; 'Jigs-med gling-pa's *rNam-mkhyen shing-rta*, p. 583. Collected Instructions (zhal-gdams) of A-'dzom 'brug-pa 'Gro-'dul-dpa'-bo-rdo-rje, vol. 3, pp. 55, 155.

38) In his *Bla-ma yang-tig*, part Wam, p. 17, Klong-chen rab-'byams-pa brings out this point very clearly:

The *sGron-ma snang-byed* states:

> The ground, initially pure since its beginningless
>   beginning
> (As) facticity, actuality and responsiveness
> Is constituted of three kinds of pristine cognitiveness.
> From it there comes a ground as the indeterminacy
>   of spontaneous givenness;
> It becomes mistaken about itself and goes astray
>   through a triple modality of loss of pure awareness,
>   four co-determinants,
> And a displacement by the cognitive capacity.

The 'triple modality of loss of pure awareness' means that the solipsistic loss is with (the pristine cognitiveness) from the very beginning, that the cognate loss of pure awareness is simultaneous (with the spontaneous givenness), and that the proliferating loss of pure awareness comes at a later stage. They are labelled differently according to their specific (forms of) loss of pure awareness. The 'four co-determinants' are the causative co-determinant or the triple modality of loss of pure awareness; the 'subjective' co-determinant is the cognitive property (of Being); the 'objective' co-determinant is the (self-)presentation (of Being), and the temporal horizon co-determinant is the above three co-determinants operating simultaneously and on the same level. 'Displacement by the cognitive capacity' means the presence of Being as individually experienced by the six kinds of sentient beings.

The reference to three kinds of pristine cognitiveness is a restatement of the basic idea in rDzogs-chen thought that Being is Awareness in a dynamic manner. In his *Vima snying-thig*, part 2, pp. 337 f, Klong-chen rab-'byams-pa speaks of the 'configurative character of the prereflective-nonthematic aspect of experience', to use modern terms. See also *mKha'-'gro yang-thig*, part 3, p. 188. The transition from the prereflective-nonthematic to the reflective-thematic in experience happens much in the same way as detailed in *Kindly Bent ot Ease Us*, part II, p. 31.

39) See also *mKha'-'gro yang-thig*, part 2, pp. 123 and 129.

40) *rNying-ma rgyud-'bum*, vol. 9, p. 577.

41) *rNying-ma rgyud-'bum*, vol. 10, p. 123.

42) This is to say, one can 'see' and one is no longer merely registering impressions.

43) These are symbols for a series of experiences. They have been detailed in *rDzogs-pa chen-po dgongs-pa zang-thal*, vol. 3, pp. 155 ff.

44) *Theg-pa'i mchog rin-po-che'i mdzod*, vol. 1, pp. 444 f.

45) *mKha'-'gro yang-thig*, part 3, p. 201; see also pp. 163 f, 179.

46) This is clearly pointed out by 'Jigs-med gling-pa in his *bDen-gnyis shing-rta*, p. 871.

47) In the history of Buddhist philosophy this has happened with the Prāsaṅgikas who claimed to convey Nāgārjuna's thought in all its purity, but ended up in stale argumentations.

48) This difference separates Buddhist metaphysics which in its conclusion remains suggestive, tentative, from Hinduist (Vedānta) metaphysics which is deductively apodictic.

49) This implies that they can never be translated mechanically on the ground that they are already there making up the vocabulary of a language. A language is a means for communicating meanings, not merely for making noises.

50) This is the *gSang-ba'i snying-po de-kho-na-nyid nges-pa* in its longer version. The quotation is found in *rNying-ma rgyud-'bum*, vol. 14, p. 76.

51) *Ngal-gso skor-gsum-gyi spyi-don legs-bshad rgya-mtsho*, p. 110.

NOTES TO CHAPTER ONE

1) The topic of this chapter, 'dreaming' (*rmi-lam*) is related to Nāgārjuna's idea of 'unorigination' (*anutpāda*, Tibetan *skye(-ba) med-pa*) by which an 'event-particle' birth is negated. Even if the adjective *ma-skyes(-pa)* is used instead of the noun, the 'thingness of thought' against which the attack is directed is not lessened.

2) The comparison with ideas in contemporary physics is not far-fetched. In rDzogs-chen texts *ngo-bo* 'facticity' is stated to be 'open-dimensional' and to have nothing to do with 'substance' and, by implication, with 'quality'. But when this term occurs in the negative form *ngo-bo-med-pa* it is used in the sense of 'having no substance' or, as one might say, 'having no mass'.

3) This is the English term for mobilité première coined by Gaston Bachelard. On its relationship to 'zero energy' and the difficulties of understanding it, see Milič Čapek, *The Philosophical Impact of Contemporary Physics*, p. 294.

4) While in the first two parts of the Trilogy Śrī Samantabhadra (*dPal Kun-tu bzang-po*) is invoked, in the third part it is Śrī Vajrasattva (*dPal rDo-rje sems-dpa'*). This difference is not without significance. The first part deals with Mind-as-such (*sems-nyid*) or, in Western philosophical terminology, Being, though not as a static thing or one contrasted with other things. The second part of the trilogy deals with Meditation (*bsam-gtan*), not so much in the sense of what a person may be doing, but rather in the sense of how man is related to Being as total meaningfulness, so that meditation is rather a mediation between Being and the human being with the emphasis on Being, total meaningfulness, complete positiveness. The third part of the trilogy emphasizes the ongoing process of Being, reaching, by the very act of soliciting, into the human being who interprets this soliciting and 'reaching-into' through his awareness of the self-presentation of Being and thereby is led 'back towards' an understanding of Being. Commenting on the term *dPal rDo-rje sems-dpa'*, Klong-chen rab-'byams-pa says in his *Ngal-gso skor-gsum-gyi spyi-don legs-bshad rgya-mtsho*, p. 111:

> *dpal* signifies the founding stratum of an engagement in a world-horizon, having five distinct components; *rdo-rje* signifies the (ultimate) founding stratum (of total meaningfulness) that does not step out of itself (into something other than itself) nor change into something other than itself; and *sems-dpa'* signifies the founding stratum of apprehendable (and appreciable) meanings variable in its indeterminateness. So it is to the Teacher—(in whom) the experience of

Buddhahood has had no beginning and will have no ending, being the arrival in the sublime citadel (of) the three founding strata (as) limpid clearness and consummate perspicacity, (symbolized by) *rDo-rje 'chang, rDo-rje sems-dpa'*, and *Kun-tu bzang-po*—that the salutation in a deep sense of dedication is made.

The 'five distinct components' indicate the facets of our experience: (a) the center from which meaning radiates into (b) its surrounding field and (c) the radiation itself which is the meaning transmitted, having (d) its own 'place' and (e) its own 'time', being not *in* space and not *in* time, but having its distinct spatiality and temporality. In *Theg-pa'i mchog rin-po-che'i mdzod*, p. 443, *rDo-rje sems-dpa'* is interpreted as *rig-pa* 'pure awareness', 'pure cognition'.

5) *ngang* signifies not a 'fixed' expanse but an utter openness which is felt and known as such because it 'grants itself' (*byin-rlabs*) as an opening-up which reaches out and this indicates the dynamic nature of Being. This 'granting itself' is the creativity (*rtsal*) of Being which proceeds as and through letting Being's light shine forth (*gdangs*).

6) Basically this verse is an elaboration of the 'invocation'. The 'dynamic reach and range' is the ultimate founding stratum of meaning, the 'majestic play', the founding stratum for the engagement in a world-horizon, and 'Mind-as-such' the founding stratum for the various apprehendable and appreciable meanings that are man's world.

7) Sūtras is the collective term for the discourses actually or imagined to have been given by the Buddha to his disciples; Tantras for works dealing with 'existential knowledge' as mediated by symbols and taught by the Buddha on the spiritual level; and Upadeśas for instructions by learned persons.

8) 'The continuum that is the Ground (or Being)' (*gzhi-dbyings*), on the one hand, indicates that there are no gaps in Being—any gaps would turn Being into isolated beings; on the other hand it lets something become manifested without becoming a thing. Again emphasis is on the dynamic nature and, as such, it creates the conditions for the actualization of all the potential

that is in man; in other words, it generates the very information that is needed for the actualization. This providing of information is 'pure (or intrinsic) awareness' (*rig-pa*), the 'mind as limpid clearness and consummate perspicacity' (*byang-chub-kyi sems*), a 'sheer lucency that has been since all beginning' (*ye-nas 'od-gsal-ba*), a 'thrust towards pleasure' (*bde-bar gshegs-pa'i snying-po*). It can be all this because its very facticity is an utter openness for which the sky can serve as an analogy, while its actuality or presence is radiance, the sun and the moon being the nearest equivalents for its light character. The ability to deal with the 'situation', to respond to what is presented, is like the bright surface of a mirror, which is not merely a passive receptor but an active revealer—that which lets the whole potential come into play. See also *rDzogs-pa chen-po sGyu-ma ngal-gso'i 'grel-pa shing-rta bzang-po*, pp. 53 f. In the following this work will be quoted in the abbreviated form *Shing-rta bzang-po*.

9) *yon-tan.* On this term see *Kindly Bent to Ease Us*, part I, p. 250, note 3. In no way does this term as used in rDzogs-chen philosophy, refer to the traditional notion of 'qualities'.

10) *lhan-cig-skyes-pa'i ma-rig-pa*, see Introduction p. 24. In his *mKha'-'gro yang-thig*, part 3, p. 117, Klong-chen rab-'byams-pa elaborates as follows:

> Before there was anything, the primordial continuum of Being in its spontaneous presence served as the ground from which (its) facticity, actuality, and responsiveness were to proceed. These three facets were not split up into separate entities. Simultaneously with the appearance of five light values (in distinct hues) which are the primary feature of the self-presentation of Being's actuality out of its facticity, there is a cognitive (response), the outward glow of Being's responsiveness. If this is recognized for what it is, it returns to its very source and becomes firmly settled as the three (existential) founding strata (of our being) which are such that they cannot be added to or subtracted from each other. Although this takes place as a spontaneous activity, it may not be recognized as Being's own light by those who

are unaware of it, and hence it is termed 'cognate loss of pure awareness', and it is termed 'loss of pure awareness proliferating into divisive concepts', in view of the addiction that holds what is self-manifesting to be something other. Together, (these 'losses') constitute the cause and the conditions (for going astray). The self-existent pristine cognitiveness that is the ultimate basic ground (Being itself) and its outward glow, five pristine cognitions (on) four founding strata (in) five hues of colored light go astray into and are mistaken for the object-area (of perceptions), the physical existence (of the perceiver), and the sense perceptions (by him). See also *ibid.,* pp. 172, 181.

11) *kun-tu brtags-pa'i ma-rig-pa.* See Introduction, p. 24, and previous note.

12) Men, gods, demi-gods, animals, spirits, denizens of hell.

13) *lta-ba.* This term not only implies vision but also a radical clearing away of all that obstructs direct vision. Creative imagination (*sgom-pa*) is the cultivation of the unobstructed vision obtained, free from all conceptual adumbrations.

14) See on this idea *Kindly Bent to Ease Us,* part I, pp. 123 ff.

15) *mnyam-rdzogs.* This combination of terms is typical for Klong-chen rab-'byams-pa. The first term, *mnyam,* refers to the problem of identity which can only be understood from the nature of identity itself, which presents itself as the 'two truths', the one conventional, the other ultimate, in the traditional parlance of Buddhist texts. 'Identity' thus becomes the relation of the ultimate 'truth' and the conventional 'truth' as a relation. In his *Shing-rta bzang-po,* pp. 61 f, Klong-chen rab-'byams-pa states: "The fact (i) that all that manifests itself in variety is such that from all beginning it has never come into being and (ii) that what incidentally manifests itself and remains from the very moment of its manifestation such that it has no reality principle—constitutes as identity the commonly accepted 'two truths'. In the specific teaching, identity is (the experience of) (iii) the founding, presenting itself as the world, as a palace, and (iv) the founded, the sentient beings as the

'content' (in the world), as deities. Through this four(-fold) identity all that is (going to be) presents itself as the Samantabhadra maṇḍala (*kun-tu bzang-po'i dkyil-'khor*). This presenting is to be imagined as having no actuality in itself but being similar to dreaming." To anyone familiar with modern philosophy the similarity with Martin Heidegger's principle of identity is obvious. The second term, *rdzogs*, indicates the fact that Being is 'complete' by not being some being.

16) The basic Guru is one's personal teacher through whom one's eyes are opened to a vision of Being. This is possible because Being speaks through him to us. As Klong-chen rab-'byams-pa indicates in his *Shing-rta bzang-po*, p. 126, the real *bla-ma rnal-'byor* (the 'tuning-in' to the Ultimate) does not admit of any concretization into any 'person' or 'deity' whatsoever. On the meaning of *bla-ma* see also *Kindly Bent to Ease Us*, part II, p. 100, note 2.

17) *ye(-nas) stong(-pa)* is a term peculiar to rDzogs-chen philosophy and may be said to point to what is best characterized as metaontological. Ontology, in the proper sense of the word, deals with Being and not with *a* being with which it is often confused. The *ye* specifically implies a 'before' all openness, before all ground. In his *Shing-rta bzang-po*, p. 153, Klong-chen rab-'byams-pa explicates this term by saying that 'since all that is has no ground, it is primarily open'. Related to this term are *babs(-kyis) stong(-pa)* and *rang-bzhin gdod* or *gzod(-ma)-nas stong(-pa)*. See below p. 132, chapter Five, note 6.

18) Practice (*sbyong*) not only implies a doing over and over again of a certain act for the sake of acquiring proficiency or skill, but even more so a process of refinement so as to become permeable to the creative forces that are the universe, to embody them, and to perceive them in the world around us.

19) These 'statuses' are felt visualizations occurring on lower levels of meditation, ranging over the world of sensuous and sensual desires and the realms of aesthetic experience, and are like cryptograms portraying the constant changes of 'psychic' life. Much of what is described in the text has its counterpart in modern psychotherapy. See Mike Samuels and Nancy Samuels, *Seeing with the Mind's Eye*, passim.

20) *'Og-min*. This term corresponds to Sanskrit Akaniṣṭha. It was interpreted as meaning either 'highest' and belonging to the 'world' as conceived in early Buddhist cosmology, or as 'invaluable' and thus descriptive of an experience. It is this latter character that prevails in rNying-ma thought. In this sense *'Og-min* reflects an 'inner landscape' whose richness varies with the levels of its experience. See Klong-chen rab-'byams-pa's commentary on the *Guhyagarbhatantra*, the *dPal gSang-ba snying-po de-kho-na-nyid nges-pa'i rgyud-kyi 'grel-pa phyogs-bcu'i mun-pa thams-cad rnam-par sel-ba*, fol. 21 a ff.

21) *don gnyis*. See *Kindly Bent to Ease Us*, part I, p. 273, note 2.

NOTES TO CHAPTER TWO

1) There is no single English term for the wide range of connotations of the Tibetan word *sgyu-ma* which more than any other term succeeds in describing sheer occurring without involving the slightest reference to a 'thing' occurring. As such it aptly illustrates Nāgārjuna's denial of an 'event–particle' cessation (*anirodha*, Tibetan *'gags-med*).

In figurative language which unfortunately has to resort to anthropomorphic imagery, Mind-as-such, which is not to be confused with *a* mind (which is a congealment of the free 'energy' that is Mind-as-such and is as 'intangible' as the 'vacuum' or 'electromagnetic wave medium' in modern atomic and quantum physics), is the great 'magician' conjuring up a welter of apparitions as intangible and elusive as their generative source.

The idea expressed by *sgyu-ma* is quite distinct from the confused and incongruous notion of *māyā* in Vedānta philosophy.

2) *khams bde-bar gshegs-pa'i snying-po*. The term *khams* is of special significance because it refers to the concrete individual as a self-regulatory system that is goal-directed, the goal being, in prosaic terms, its optimum performance. The system's process passes through different levels, each of which represents a specific value organization. The three levels are those of an unregenerate person, of a Bodhisattva, and of a Buddha. Each of the levels also represents a state of, as well as a basis for,

further refinement. The thrust towards well(-being) (*bde-ba*) indicates that 'pleasure' (*bde-ba*) is basic to health, whether we understand health in terms of the body or the mind. Just as illness is loss of health so any decline in pleasure represents a lowered state of well-being. Hence, an unregenerate person who is in the grip of his emotions is in a rather poor state of health, 'out of sorts' or, as the texts say, 'impure' (*ma-dag-pa*). A Bodhisattva, ethical man, is on the way to recovery (recovering from a state of poor health and re-discovering his health or humanity), and hence is 'both impure and pure' (*ma-dag-dag-pa*). A Buddha is one who is whole and healthy in every respect and hence 'thoroughly pure' (*shin-tu rnam-dag*). See *Shing-rta bzang-po*, p. 85. The triple gradation in terms of 'purity' has found its concise exposition in the *Mahāyānottaratantraśāstra* I 47.

3) *rang-bzhin med-pa*. The translation of this term here is based on 'Jigs-med gling-pa's interpretation. See his *rNam-mkhyen shing-rta*, p. 684.

4) See also note 8 to Chapter One.

5) They are desire and attachment, aversion and hatred, and indifference and obtuseness. See also *Kindly Bent to Ease Us*, part I, p. 54.

6) See also note 15 to Chapter One.

7) *rig-sngags*. In particular, this term emphasizes the 'active' aspect as contrasted with the 'appreciative' (*gzungs-sngags*) one, inherent in the dynamic of Being, the unity of 'action' and 'appreciation' being the great mystery of Being (*gsang-sngags*). On this triple division of *sngags* see 'Jigs-med gling-pa's *rNam-mkhyen shing-rta*, p. 29.

8) 'Freedom' is synonymous with 'Being'. While 'Being' is an ontological concept leading beyond ontology in the traditional Western sense, 'freedom' is the manner in which 'Being' is always present dynamically. Insofar as Being is cognitive (and not merely an object of subjective cognition) its freedom is not some entity to be reached or chosen in a predetermined way which destroys the very idea of freedom before it is allowed to

operate; it is more a freedom of understanding. It has been dealt with exhaustively in all its subtle nuances in rDzogs-chen works, while only a tentative step in the direction of 'freedom', releasing it from its reductionist travesty, has been made in Western philosophy under the impact of existentialism. See, for instance, John Wild, *Existence and the World of Freedom.*

9) It comprises the thirty-seven facets as detailed in *Kindly Bent to Ease Us,* part I, pp. 241.

10) On this topic see *Kindly Bent to Ease Us,* part I, p. 252 note 7.

11) This is the interdependence of twelve links in the chain of becoming. Each of them is open to different interpretations, depending on the hierarchical level on which they happen to operate. See, for instance, *mKha'-'gro yang-thig,* part 2, pp. 175 ff.

12) In his *Shing-rta bzang-po,* p. 120, Klong-chen rab-'byams-pa likens the spells of a magician, whereby pebbles appear as horses and so on, to the actions of sentient beings assuming different statuses. In the same way as the magic horses are but an apparition exerting an enchanting effect on the observer, so also the world process is but an apparition to the observer who is part of this display of apparitions.

13) In his *Shing-rta bzang-po,* pp. 121 f Klong-chen rab-'byams-pa specifies those who are thus to be pitied. They are the non-Buddhists—who are fettered tightly by emotions that burn like fire, by obstacles set up by deadening (spiritual) forces, by emotions and opinions—but also Buddhists who are attached to the pleasurable feelings that prevail in meditative states, as well as the beginners among Śrāvakas, Pratyeka-buddhas and Bodhisattvas.

14) In his *Shing-rta bzang-po,* p. 125, Klong-chen rab-'byams-pa associates the wizardry that comes with the sense of meaningfulness, with pure awareness as mind (moving in the direction of) limpid clearness and consummate perspicacity: "there is nothing—be this the 'pure' as at the time of Buddhahood or the 'impure', the mistaken presentation and mistaken notions at the time of Saṃsāra—that does not come under 'loss of pure awareness'. To conceive of something as good is (the

operation of) 'pure awareness', to conceive of something as evil also is (the operation of) 'pure awareness'. What presents itself in various forms is nothing other than what presents itself to 'pure awareness', hence all pure awareness has to do with meaningfulness. Just as space is neither good nor bad, regardless of whether it is found in a jug of clay or in one of gold, each of which presents itself as a good or bad container respectively, so also, although Saṃsāra and Nirvāṇa may present themselves as good or bad, (their) presentation to 'pure awareness' must be known as being neither good nor bad." In other words, it is only in the thematic, reflective phase of experience that judgments occur and distort the immediacy of experience.

15) As Klong-chen rab-'byams-pa points out in his *Shing-rta bzang-po*, p. 126, the keynote of the exercise is 'devotedness', not the content of the exercise, because any fixation on the 'what' could prevent the person from becoming free. The content is merely a challenge to 'look deeper'.

16) To regain one's Being, one must stay in the intermediate state between the daytime enchantment of the phenomenal world being there and yet nothing and the night time enchantment of the 'divine' realms of one's dreams.

Notes to Chapter Three

1) 'Illusion' (*mig-yor*) is used by Klong-chen rab-'byams-pa to illustrate Nāgārjuna's denial of an 'event-particle' coming ⊀(*anāgama*, Tibetan *'ong-ba med-pa*), illustrating the thingness of thought so prevalent in Eastern and Western thinking, as summed up by David Hume in his *Treatise on Human Nature*, part IV§4: "The idea of motion necessarily supposes that of a body moving." On the modern conception of motion ('coming' and 'going' in picturesque language), see Milič Čapek, *The Philosophical Impact of Contemporary Physics*, pp. 262 ff.

2) *med-(bzhin) snang-(ba)*, also *med-pa gsal-snang*, sums up the very nature of experience as a dynamic process having a dual character and movement. The term *med-pa*, which in ordinary par-

lance denotes the negation of a particular being as when we say 'there is no mountain' and which can be extended to include the negation of *any* thing, is in the above combination not used in its contrast with the assertion that there is something (*yod-pa*) as when we say 'there is a mountain', rather it indicates the prereflective nonthematic side of experience, which is the component of experience as yet undisturbed by explicit reflection on what is found in experience. But as the term *bzhin* indicates, the 'prereflective' component does not precede the reflective component, either genetically or historically. The prereflective nonthematic *continues* into the reflective-thematic (*snang-ba*). As 'experience' this interwovenness of two structured features comes as a play, as Klong-chen rab-'byams-pa states in his *Tshig-don rin-po-che'i mdzod*, p. 246. This theme of 'there being nothing and yet there being a lucid presence' (which would be a very literal translation) occurs over and over again in Klong-chen rab-'byams-pa's *Lung-gi gter mdzod*, his own commentary on his *rDzogs-pa chen-po Chos-dbyings rin-po-che'i mdzod*. For a penetrating analysis of experience in Western philosophy see Calvin O. Schrag, *Experience and Being*, pp. 45 f, 90.

3) In his *Shing-rta bzang-po*, pp. 132 f, Klong-chen rab-'byams-pa gives the following explanation to this stanza:

In the same manner as a solid object may cast a shadow that is similar to, but not identical with, it, so also the self-effulgence of the primordial cognitive property of the continuum of Being, that comes as the spontaneous givenness in openness and radiance, seems to have a certain form about which (the process) by not recognizing itself for what it is, becomes mistaken and strays into the subject-object dichotomy. There thus come five psychophysical constituents, five elemental forces, five emotions, the five senses and so on, in the course which the self-effulgence of the cognitive property (of Being) takes. It is through the presence of these various mistaken presentations of dissimilar affective processes, of the resilience of the concrete, of impure observable qualities, of karmic activities and emotional imbalances that the six kinds of sentient beings in the three realms of existence move around in Saṃsāra by creating their individual conditions for existence.

4) *gdod-ma'i chos-nyid.* As Klong-chen rab-'byams-pa points out in his *Shing-rta bzang-po,* p. 135 *gdod-ma* is synonymous with the 'openness of Being', and is not to be understood in any temporal sense. The dual character of experience is again emphasized:

> Although (some topic) is present in the thematic component of individual experience (*so-so rang-gi rig-ngor*), it is not so in the non-thematic component (*gshis-ngor*), but his does not mean any temporal priority.

chos-nyid is used to indicate the 'internal logic' of Being as a process. The universe is not an array of lifeless 'things' but an interplay of 'meanings' and as such has its 'meaningfulness'.

5) *nyams rtogs.* The former is likened to smoke, the latter to fire. Out of the 'understanding' (*rtogs*) of the open dimension of cognitiveness comes the 'feeling' ('experience') of what is meant by pleasure, radiance, non-dividedness. Real understanding makes a person 'feel' for what he understands. *Shing-rta bzang-po,* p. 140.

Notes to Chapter Four

1) 'Mirage' (*smig-rgyu*) is used to illustrate Nāgārjuna's denial of an 'event-particle' going (*anirgama,* Tibetan *'gro-ba med-pa*). For the reasoning behind this negation see also note 1 to Chapter Three.

2) See note 2 to Chapter Three. In his *Shing-rta bzang-po,* p. 144, Klong-chen rab-'byams-pa restates this idea by saying that whatever comes as 'external and internal' meanings and is concretized into the entities of the 'world out there' and the 'ideas and feelings in here', is a self-effulgence of Being that retains its primordial openness. As to 'primordial' see also note 4 to Chapter Three.

3) *gzungs.* Klong-chen rab-'byams-pa explains this term as meaning not to let slip from memory. *Shing-rta bzang-po,* p. 146.

Notes to Chapter Five

1) 'The reflection of the moon in water' (*chu-zla*) is used to bring out the specific character of 'presence', which cannot simply be dismissed. It is related to Nāgārjuna's denial of a state of ultimate extinction (*anuccheda*, Tibetan *chad-pa med-pa*).

2) In his *Shing-rta bzang-po*, p. 148, Klong-chen rab-'byams-pa elaborates the image as follows:

> In the center of a lake that is the intrinsically pure Mind-as-such, the site for the unity of 'existentiality' and 'cogni-tiveness', which is such that the one cannot be detracted from nor added to the other as separate entities, has been from the very beginning with (the ground of Being) as the spontaneous givenness of Being in which the Buddha qual-ities are as numerous as the grains of sand in the river Ganges. This is made the pool (of individual experience) by the cognate loss of pure awareness and by the waves that are churned up as subject and object by the proliferating loss of pure awareness; the capabilities of the continuum of Being, that are (like) the bright stars, do not shine brightly, but by the power of karmic actions and emotional imbalance they shine brightly as mistaken identities, whereby one moves from one round of existence into another.

3) The text takes color-form as an example for the five perceptual situations, i.e., the five ordinary sense operations and the sixth, the thought situation.

4) *Shing-rta bzang-po*, pp. 150 f: "They are a mere (presence-) presentation; nothing factual is found; observability does not cease; the mistaken presence is the paradox of there being nothing and yet there being a presence. Because of this para-doxical character they are 'nothing', and because they are merely a display of imagery they are 'vain and hollow'; be-cause they are there without having any truth in them they are 'delusive'; and because they have no hard core they are like a 'plantain'. Know this presence of open-dimensional imagery to be a mere play."

5) Being as a 'continuum' is an undisrupted vastness and it cannot be 'fragmented'. If it could be split up it would lose its very being and become reduced to a partial aspect of itself.

6) *Shing-rta bzang-po*, p. 153: Since all that is has been such that it cannot be reduced to a ground, it has been nothing as such from the very beginning (*ye-nas stong-pa*); since they have nothing factual about them, they are nothing by virtue of the non-occurrence of sedimentation (*babs-kyis stong-pa*); and since they have no defining characteristics as such, they have been nothing as such in their actuality or existential immediacy (*rang-bzhin gzod-ma-nas stong-pa*).

NOTES TO CHAPTER SIX

1) The image of an 'echo' (*brag-cha*) aptly illustrates a process and is less concerned with a particular existent or 'thing' in the broadest sense of the word. Although the image is used to elaborate Nāgārjuna's denial of a property 'lastingness' (*aśāśvata*—the Sanskrit word is an adjective, not a noun) the Tibetan interpreter understood it as a denial of a particular existent (*rtag-pa med-pa*) and not as a description of something in negative terms (*mi-rtag-pa*) 'impermanent'. This may well reflect a difference in thinking: 'process'-thinking with the Tibetans and 'thing'-thinking with the Indians. 'Thing'-thinking is prone to argumentation. This distinction between two kinds of thinking does not involve an unbridgeable gulf between them, rather it indicates dominant traits.

2) In his *Shing-rta bzang-po*, p. 160, Klong-chen rab-'byams-pa elaborates on this stanza in terms of rDzogs-chen philosophy:

> The actuality (existential immediacy, *rang-bzhin*) which has no facticity (*ngo-bo-med-pa*) (other than) the primordial ground, open and radiant, is made the condition (for mistaken identification) by the cognate loss of pure awareness and the (proliferating) loss of awareness operating on the same level as the cognate one. The mistaken (presence-) presentation, that arises from the self-effulgence of the self-presentation of Being, appears as Saṃsāra, similar to an echo, since the cognitive response and nothing else presents itself as a thereness without there being anything. But this is actually nothing else but a (presence-)presentation of what is not in a lucent immediacy.

3) The 'coarse' level comprises all that we understand by the external world and the thoughts we harbor about it; the 'subtle' is the qualities that go with the coarse. *Shing-rta bzang-po*, p. 161.

4) In his *Shing-rta bzang-po*, p. 164, Klong-chen rab-'byams-pa explains the descriptive terms as follows:

Since all that presents itself as object cannot be grasped and taken hold of, it is elusive; since it has no solid core, it is tenuous; since there is nothing and yet there is a presence, it is paradoxical; since to what one might hold has slipped away, it is evasive; since it has nothing to last it is casual.

5) This German word, better than any other term, captures the character of what comes about through the exercise of non-interference. See, in particular on this topic, Calvin O. Schrag, *Experience and Being*, pp. 112 f.

NOTES TO CHAPTER SEVEN

1) 'Cloud-land' (*dri-za'i grong-khyer*) has here been used to illustrate Nāgārjuna's denial of the property of difference (*anānārtha*). As the Tibetan interpretation indicates, *tha-dad ma-yin-pa* describes in negative terms, but does not deny 'existence'. On this difference see Introduction, p. 30.

2) Alexander Gosztonyi, *Grundlagen der Erkenntnis*, p. 68, distinguishes three characteristics of our senses: reality value (indicative of the degree to which a sense transmits material resistance), formal evidence value (indicative of the degree of insight into formal relationships), and existential evidence value (indicative of the intensity of the experience of 'existence'). See also Erich Jantsch, *Design for Evolution*, p. 134.

3) In his *Shing-rta bzang-po*, p. 173, Klong-chen rab-'byams-pa deals with the identity (non-duality) of Saṃsāra and Nirvāṇa. Identity for him is not an equation. His words are:

The cause for Saṃsāra lies in the five emotions, together with the proliferation of divisive concepts. If these are investigated as to their continuous presence without there being anything (of this kind), (we realize) that they have nothing about them (which would allow us to speak of their facticity as something) at all. The same applies to Mind-as-such. These two features are not two in the open (dimension of Being) that, therefore, has no actuality (as existential immediacy) as such. This is what is meant by the non-duality of Saṃsāra and Nirvāṇa.

NOTES TO CHAPTER EIGHT

1) 'Phantom' (*sprul-pa*) illustrates Nāgārjuna's denial of the property of identity (*anekārtha*). The Tibetan interpretation also stresses the character of non-singularity (*gcig-tu ma-yin-pa, gcig-tu ma-grub-pa*). Like *sgyu-ma* (see above, Chapter Two note 1), the term *sprul-pa* presents considerable difficulties for rendering it adequately in English. The choice of 'phantom' is based on the consideration that this term is related in meaning to 'apparition' which often implies suddenness and unexpectedness as found in a magic (*sgyu-ma*) show, and also to 'dreaming' (*rmi-lam*), having no substance or matter. Apart from these connotations, *sprul-pa* also may mean 'fancy' as the power to conceive and give expression to images that may seem far removed from 'reality' and yet may anticipate empirical discoveries. In the broadest sense of the word, *sprul-pa* is the process of the (human) mind as it manifests itself projected into an environment.

2) This distinction between mind (*sems*), a noetic-noematic complex, and pristine cognitiveness (*ye-shes*) is basic to rDzogs-chen thought. It does not imply a dualism in which its two sides are irreconcilable, but merely focusses on the dual nature of experience as a continuum of reflective-thematic (*sems*) and prereflective nonthematic (*ye-shes*) operations that remain interwoven. The *sGyu-'phrul dra-ba* is a work or, rather a collection of works highly appreciated by the followers of the rNying-ma tradition.

3) For the 'three poisons' see note 5 to Chapter Two. The 'five poisons' are the above three with 'anger' and 'jealousy' added.

4) See on these 'forces' *Kindly Bent to Ease Us*, part I, p. 259 and part II, p. 18.

5) On these stages see in particular *Kindly Bent to Ease Us*, part II, pp. 44 f.

6) On these control centers see *Kindly Bent to Ease Us*, part II, pp. 15 ff. The highly 'technical' language employed in this passage points to the harmonic interplay between the various levels of organization by which the living person comes to know himself in his enigmatic participation in 'matter' and 'spirit'. 'Motility' (*rlung*), as well as its 'pathways' (*rtsa*) constituting certain flow-patterns, can be 'seen' and 'felt' concretely. But to attend to these visualizations and feelings is a 'coarse' or low-level technique which in certain cases may be necessary and appropriate. In the picturesque language of Klong-chen rab-'byams-pa, it may be necessary to break a horse ('motility') to the rein so that the rider ('mind-mentation') may enjoy his ride over his domain (*khams*, 'the psycho-physical make-up'). However, the important point is to go beyond this 'visible' realm by understanding what is going on. Such understanding proceeds from higher-level organizations and more stable regimes, indicated by 'control centers'.

The process of purification is to recognize what is going on for what it is and not to distort it by ego-centered interferences. As such it takes place on, and is grounded in, the cognitive property of Being (*rig-pa*) and thus purifies and, in this purification, transmutes 'desires' into pure pleasure, 'aversion' into holistic feelings, 'obtuseness' into sheer lucency, and 'arrogance-jealousy' and the other 'emotions' most strongly associated with the ego into charismatic activities. *Shing-rta bzang-po*, pp. 201 ff.

Index*

TECHNICAL TERMS

Tibetan

---

*This cumulative index includes references from all three volumes of
"The Trilogy of Finding Comfort and Ease."

Sanskrit

NAMES AND SUBJECTS

THE BUDDHA: LIVES AND TEACHINGS

Dhammapada
The Fortunate Aeon (Bhadrakalpika Sūtra)
Leaves of the Heaven Tree
The Marvelous Companion: Āryaśūra's Jātakamālā
Voice of the Buddha (Lalitavistara Sūtra)
Wisdom of Buddha (Saṁdhinirmocana Sūtra)

BIOGRAPHY / HISTORY

Buddha's Lions, by Abhayadatta
The Legend of the Great Stupa, by Padmasambhava
The Life and Liberation of Padmasambhava
Mother of Knowledge, by Nam-mkha'i sNying-po

ABHIDHARMA

The Arthaviniścaya Sūtra and Commentary
Mind in Buddhist Psychology, by Yeshe Gyaltsen

MAHAYANA TEACHINGS

Invitation to Enlightenment, by Mātṛceṭa and Candragomin
Master of Wisdom: Six Texts by Nāgārjuna

MEDITATION / BODHISATTVA PRACTICE

Calm and Clear, by Lama Mipham
Kindly Bent to Ease Us, by Longchenpa
Path of Heroes, by Zhechen Gyaltshab

POETRY AND DRAMA

Elegant Sayings
Golden Zephyr
Joy for the World (Candragomin's Lokānanda)